Survival Communications in Texas: Big Bend Region

John E. Parnell, KK4HWX

13 ISBN 978-1477478486
10 ISBN 1477478485

Cover design by:
Lynda Colón
FREELANCE GRAPHIC DESIGN &
MARKETING COMMUNICATIONS
www.hirelynda.webs.com

I do wish to acknowledge the hard work of **Angie Shirley** in putting together the database required for this book. Without her efforts, this book could not have been done.

Titles available in this series:

Survival Communications in Alabama
Survival Communications in Alaska
Survival Communications in Arizona
Survival Communications in Arkansas
Survival Communications in California
Survival Communications in Colorado
Survival Communications in Connecticut
Survival Communications in Delaware
Survival Communications in Florida
Survival Communications in Georgia
Survival Communications in Hawaii
Survival Communications in Idaho
Survival Communications in Illinois
Survival Communications in Indiana
Survival Communications in Iowa
Survival Communications in Kansas
Survival Communications in Kentucky
Survival Communications in Louisiana
Survival Communications in Maine
Survival Communications in Maryland
Survival Communications in Massachusetts
Survival Communications in Michigan
Survival Communications in Minnesota
Survival Communications in Mississippi
Survival Communications in Missouri
Survival Communications in Montana
Survival Communications in Nebraska

Survival Communications in Nevada
Survival Communications in New Hampshire
Survival Communications in New Jersey
Survival Communications in New Mexico
Survival Communications in New York
Survival Communications in North Carolina
Survival Communications in North Dakota
Survival Communications in Ohio
Survival Communications in Oklahoma
Survival Communications in Oregon
Survival Communications in Pennsylvania
Survival Communications in Rhode Island
Survival Communications in South Carolina
Survival Communications in South Dakota
Survival Communications in Tennessee
Survival Communications in Texas
Survival Communications in Utah
Survival Communications in Vermont
Survival Communications in Virginia
Survival Communications in Washington
Survival Communications in West Virginia
Survival Communications in Wisconsin
Survival Communications in Wyoming

The above titles are available from your favorite online or brick-and-mortar bookstore or directly from the publisher at Tutor Turtle Press LLC, 1027 S. Pendleton St. – Suite B-10, Easley, SC 29642.

TABLE OF CONTENTS

Appendix A – Texas Ham Radio Clubs

Amateur and Ham Radio Clubs – By City

Appendix B – Texan Ham Licensees by City in the Big Bend Region

Cities and Towns in the Big Bend Region of Texas

x

Survival Communications in Texas: Big Bend Region

Perhaps you have prepared for WTSHTF or TEOTWAWKI with respect to food, water, self-defense and shelter. But what about communication?

Whenever there is a disaster (hurricane, earthquake, economic collapse, nuclear war, EMF, solar eruption, etc.), the normal means of communication that we're all reliant upon (cell phone, land line phone, the Internet, etc.) will probably be, at best, sporadic and at worst, non-existent.

As this author sees it, short of smoke signals and mirrors, there are three options for communication in "trying times": (1) GMRS or FRS radios; (2) CB radios; and (3) ham or amateur radio. Let's consider each of these options to come up with the most acceptable one.

GMRS (General Mobile Radio Service) / FRS (Family Radio Service)

GMRS (General Mobile Radio Service) / FRS (Family Radio Service) radios work optimally over short distances where there is minimal interference. Originally designed to be used as pagers, particularly inside a building or other such confined area, these radios are low-cost and convenient to carry. Unfortunately their small size and light weight comes with a trade-off – short range and short battery life. These radios are supposed to be able to communicate for up to 25-30 miles. Right. That's on level terrain, without buildings or trees getting in the way. While battery life technology is constantly improving, you will need spare batteries to keep communicating or someway of recharging the ones in the radio. In this author's opinion, GMRS/FRS radios are not first choice when concerned with medium or long range communication.

CB (Citizens Band)

CB (Citizens Band) radios operate in a frequency range originally reserved for ham or amateur radio operation. Because of the overwhelming number of people wishing quick, low-cost, regulation-free communication, the FCC (Federal Communication Commission) split off a portion of the frequency spectrum and allowed anyone to purchase a CB radio and start communicating. No test. No license. Just personal/business communication. Today, CB radios are readily available in such outlets as eBay and Craigslist. This author has seen them at yard/garage/tag sales and at flea markets.

CB radios come in a variety of "flavors." Fixed units, sometimes referred to as base units are intended for home use. For the most part, they derive their power from the utility company. In the event of loss of electricity, most base units can also be connected to a 12-volt battery, like that in your car/truck. If you choose to obtain a fixed unit, make sure you know how to connect the unit to the battery – ahead of time. Trying to figure this out when you're under extra stress is not a good situation.

A second type of CB radio is designed to be mobile, that is, installed in your car/truck. It gets its power from the vehicle's battery. You can either attach an antenna permanently to the vehicle or have a removable, magnetic type antenna.

The third type of CB radio is designed for handheld use. They are small and light. Most weigh less than a pound and operate on batteries. Yes, using batteries in a CB poses the same limitations as those by the GMRS/FRS radios, but have the added advantage that most handheld units come with a cigarette lighter adapter. Comes in handy when you are on the move and wish to be able to communicate both from a vehicle and also when you have to abandon it.

While they have a greater range than GMRS/FRS radios, CB radios are, legally, limited to operate on 40 channels, with a power rating of four (4) watts or less. Yes, it is possible to alter CB radios to get around these limitations, but not legally,

Ham/Amateur Radio

Ham/Amateur radio is very appealing. With a ham radio, you are not limited to less than 50 miles, but can communicate with anyone in the world (who also has access to a ham radio, of course).

Standardized Amateur Radio Prepper Communications Plan

In the event of a nationwide catastrophic disaster, the nationwide network of Amateur Radio licensed preppers will need a set of standardized meeting frequencies to share information and coordinate activities between various prepper groups. This Standardized Amateur Radio Communications Plan establishes a set of frequencies on the 80 meter, 40 meter, 20 meter, and 2 meter Amateur Radio bands for use during these types of catastrophic disasters.

Routine nets will not be held on all of these frequencies, but preppers are encouraged to use them when coordinating with other preppers on a routine basis. Routine nets may be conducted by The American Preparedness Radio Net (TAPRN) on these or other frequencies as they see fit. However, TAPRN will promote the use of these standardized frequencies by all Amateur Radio licensed preppers during times of catastrophic disaster. The promotion of this Standardized Amateur Radio Communications Plan is encouraged by all means within the prepper community, including via Amateur Radio, Twitter, Facebook, and various blogs.

Standardized Frequencies and Modes
80 Meters – 3.818 MHz LSB (TAPRN Net: Sundays at 9 PM ET)
40 Meters – 7.242 MHz LSB
40 Meters Morse Code / Digital – 7.073 MHz USB (TAPRN: Sundays at 7:30 PM ET on CONTESTIA 4/250)
20 Meters – 14.242 MHz USB
2 Meters – 146.420 MHz FM

Nets and Network Etiquette

In times of nationwide catastrophic disaster, the ability of any one prepper to initiate and sustain themselves as a net control may be limited by the availability of power and other resource shortages. However, all licensed preppers are encouraged to maintain a listening watch on these frequencies as often as possible during a catastrophic disaster. Preppers may routinely announce themselves in the following manner:

• This is [Your Callsign Phonetically] in [Your State], maintaining a listening watch on [Standard Frequency] for any preppers on frequency seeking information or looking to provide information. Please call [Your Callsign Phonetically]. Preppers exchanging information that may require follow up should agree upon a designated time to return to the frequency and provide further information. If other stations are utilizing the frequency at the designated time you return, maintain watch and proceed with your communications when those stations are finished. If your communications are urgent and the stations on frequency are not passing information of a critical nature, interrupt with the word "Break" and request use of the frequency.

For More Information

Catastrophe Network: http://www.catastrophenetwork.org or @CatastropheNet on Twitter The American Preparedness Radio Network: http://www.taprn.com or @TAPRN on Twitter

© 2011 Catastrophe Network, Please Distribute Freely

In order to use a ham radio, legally, one must be licensed to do so by the FCC (other countries have analogous governmental bodies to regulate ham radio). To obtain a license is quite easy – take a test and pay your license fee. There are currently three classes of license – Technician, General, and Amateur Extra. With each of these licenses come specific abilities.

Technician class is the beginning level. The exam consists of 35 multiple choice questions randomly drawn from a pool of 395 questions. The question pool is readily available online for free downloading (http://www.ncvec.org/downloads/Revised%20Element%202.Pdf) or in such publications at *Ham Radio License Manual Revised 2nd Edition* (ISBN 978-0-87259-097-7). The current Technician pool of questions is to be used from July 1, 2010 to June 30, 2014. Be sure the question pool you are studying from is current. You will need to score at least 26 correct to pass. (Do not worry, Morse Code is no longer on the test, although many ham operators use it anyway.) You do not need to take a formal class in order to qualify to take the exam. You can learn the material on your own. Most people spend 10-15 hours studying and then successfully take the exam. The cost of taking the exam is under $20. The exam is given in MANY locations throughout the US. Usually the exam is given by area ham clubs. You do not have to belong to the club to take the exam. Check Appendix A for a listing of clubs in South Carolina.

Topics for the Technician License in Amateur Radio

The Technician license exam covers such topics as basic regulations, operating practices, and electronic theory, with a focus on VHF and UHF applications. Below is the syllabus for the Technician Class.

Subelement T1 – FCC Rules, descriptions and definitions for the amateur radio service, operator and station license responsibilities

[6 Exam Questions – 6 Groups]

T1A – Amateur Radio services; purpose of the amateur service, amateur-satellite service, operator/primary station license grant, where FCC rules are codified, basis and purpose of FCC rules, meanings of basic terms used in FCC rules

T1B – Authorized frequencies; frequency allocations, ITU regions, emission type, restricted sub-bands, spectrum sharing, transmissions near band edges

T1C – Operator classes and station call signs; operator classes, sequential, special event, and vanity call sign systems, international communications, reciprocal operation, station license licensee, places where the amateur service is regulated by the FCC, name and address on ULS, license term, renewal, grace period

T1D – Authorized and prohibited transmissions

T1E – Control operator and control types; control operator required, eligibility, designation of control operator, privileges and duties, control point, local, automatic and remote control, location of control operator

T1F – Station identification and operation standards; special operations for repeaters and auxiliary stations, third party communications, club stations, station security, FCC inspection

Subelement T2 – Operating Procedures

[3 Exam Questions – 3 Groups]

T2A – Station operation; choosing an operating frequency, calling another station, test transmissions, use of minimum power, frequency use, band plans

T2B – VHF/UHF operating practices; SSB phone, FM repeater, simplex, frequency offsets, splits and shifts, CTCSS, DTMF, tone squelch, carrier squelch, phonetics

T2C – Public service; emergency and non-emergency operations, message traffic handling

Subelement T3 – Radio wave characteristics, radio and electromagnetic properties, propagation modes

[3 Exam Questions – 3 Groups]

T3A – Radio wave characteristics; how a radio signal travels; distinctions of HF, VHF and UHF; fading, multipath; wavelength vs. penetration; antenna orientation

T3B – Radio and electromagnetic wave properties; the electromagnetic spectrum, wavelength vs. frequency, velocity of electromagnetic waves

T3C – Propagation modes; line of sight, sporadic E, meteor, aurora scatter, tropospheric ducting, F layer skip, radio horizon

Subelement T4 - Amateur radio practices and station setup

[2 Exam Questions – 2 Groups]

T4A – Station setup; microphone, speaker, headphones, filters, power source, connecting a computer, RF grounding

T4B – Operating controls; tuning, use of filters, squelch, AGC, repeater offset, memory channels

Subelement T5 – Electrical principles, math for electronics, electronic principles, Ohm's Law

[4 Exam Questions – 4 Groups]

T5A – Electrical principles; current and voltage, conductors and insulators, alternating and direct current

T5B – Math for electronics; decibels, electronic units and the metric system

T5C – Electronic principles; capacitance, inductance, current flow in circuits, alternating current, definition of RF, power calculations

T5D – Ohm's Law

Subelement T6 – Electrical components, semiconductors, circuit diagrams, component functions

[4 Exam Groups – 4 Questions]

T6A – Electrical components; fixed and variable resistors, capacitors, and inductors; fuses, switches, batteries

T6B – Semiconductors; basic principles of diodes and transistors

T6C – Circuit diagrams; schematic symbols

T6D – Component functions

Subelement T7 – Station equipment, common transmitter and receiver problems, antenna measurements and troubleshooting, basic repair and testing

[4 Exam Questions – 4 Groups]

T7A – Station radios; receivers, transmitters, transceivers

T7B – Common transmitter and receiver problems; symptoms of overload and overdrive, distortion, interference, over and under modulation, RF feedback, off frequency signals; fading and noise; problems with digital communications interfaces

T7C – Antenna measurements and troubleshooting; measuring SWR, dummy loads, feedline failure modes

T7D – Basic repair and testing; soldering, use of a voltmeter, ammeter, and ohmmeter

Subelement T8 – Modulation modes, amateur satellite operation, operating activities, non-voice communications

[4 Exam Questions – 4 Groups]

T8A – Modulation modes; bandwidth of various signals

T8B – Amateur satellite operation; Doppler shift, basic orbits, operating protocols

T8C – Operating activities; radio direction finding, radio control, contests, special event stations, basic linking over Internet

T8D – Non-voice communications; image data, digital modes, CW, packet, PSK31

Subelement T9 – Antennas, feedlines

[2 Exam Groups – 2 Questions]

T9A – Antennas; vertical and horizontal, concept of gain, common portable and mobile antennas, relationships between antenna length and frequency

T9B – Feedlines; types, losses vs. frequency, SWR concepts, matching, weather protection, connectors

Subelement T0 – AC power circuits, antenna installation, RF hazards

[3 Exam Questions – 3 Groups]

T0A – AC power circuits; hazardous voltages, fuses and circuit breakers, grounding, lightning protection, battery safety, electrical code compliance

T0B – Antenna installation; tower safety, overhead power lines

T0C – RF hazards; radiation exposure, proximity to antennas, recognized safe power levels, exposure to others

Once your name and call sign are available in the FCC database, you have the privilege of operating on all VHF (2 m) and UHF (70 cm) frequencies above 30 megahertz (MHz) and HF frequencies 80, 40, and 15 meter, and on the 10 meter band using Morse code (CW), voice, and digital mode. For a Technician license in Texas, your call sign will consist of a two-letter prefix beginning with K or W, the number five (5), and a three-letter suffix. The single digit number in the call sign is determined according to which area of the US you obtain your first license. Even though you may move to another state, you keep this number in your call sign. This is also true should you upgrade to a higher license and get a new call sign. The numeral portion of your call sign stays the same.

Call Sign Numbers

Below is a chart showing the various numbers and the state(s) in which you would obtain the number.

Call Sign Number	State(s)
0	CO, IA, KS, MN, MO, NE, ND, SD
1	CT, ME, MA, NH, RI, VT
2	NJ, NY
3	DE, DC, MD, PA
4	AL, FL, GA, KY, NC, SC, TN, VA
5	AR, LA, MS, NM, OK, TX
6	CA
7	AZ, ID, MT, NV, OR, WA, UT, WY
8	MI, OH, WV
9	IL, IN, WI

Residents of Alaska may have any of the following call sign prefixes assigned to them: AL0-7, KL0-7, NL0-7, or WL0-7. Likewise, residents of Hawaii may have the prefix AH6-7, KH6-7, NH6-7, or WH6-7 assigned.

Once you obtain your Technician license, do not stop there. Go and get your General license.

General is the second of three ham license classes. Like the Technician license, to get a General license, you merely have to take a 35-question multiple choice exam and pay your license fee. Passing is still at least 26 correct answers and the fee is the same (less than $20). Again the question pool is available for free online (http://www.ncvec.org/page.php?id=358). It is also available in such print publications as *The ARRL General Class License Manual 7th Edition* (ISBN 978-0-87259-811-9). The current General pool of questions is to be used from July 1, 2011 to June 30, 2015. Be sure the question pool you are using is current. Being a bit more comprehensive than the Technician license, the General license usually requires 15-20 hours of study to learn the material. Check Appendix A for a listing of clubs in South Carolina where you might take your exam. Once your name and NEW call sign is listed in the FCC database, you're good to go. For a General license in Texas, your call sign will consist of a one-letter prefix beginning with K, N or W, the number five (5), and a three-letter suffix.

Topics for the General License in Amateur Radio

The General license exam covers regulations, operating practices and electronic theory. Below is the syllabus for the General Class.

Subelement G1 – Commission's Rules

(5 Exam Questions – 5 Groups)
G1A – General Class control operator frequency privileges; primary and secondary allocations
G1B – Antenna structure limitations; good engineering and good amateur practice, beacon operation; restricted operation; retransmitting radio signals
G1C – Transmitter power regulations; data emission standards
G1D – Volunteer Examiners and Volunteer Examiner Coordinators; temporary identification
G1E – Control categories; repeater regulations; harmful interference; third party rules; ITU regions

---

Subelement G2 – Operating procedures

(5 Exam Questions – 5 Groups)
G2A – Phone operating procedures; USB/LSB utilization conventions; procedural signals; breaking into a OSO in progress; VOX operation
G2B – Operating courtesy; band plans, emergencies, including drills and emergency communications
G2C – CW operating procedures and procedural signals; Q signals and common abbreviations; full break in
G2D – Amateur Auxiliary; minimizing interference; HF operations

G2E – Digital operating; procedures, procedural signals and common abbreviations

Subelement G3 – Radio wave propagation

(3 Exam Questions – 3 Groups)

G3A – Sunspots and solar radiation; ionospheric disturbances; propagation forecasting and indices

G3B – Maximum Usable Frequency; Lowest Usable Frequency; propagation

G3C – Ionospheric layers; critical angle and frequency; HF scatter; Near Vertical Incidence Sky waves

Subelement G4 – Amateur radio practices

(5 Exam Questions – 5 Groups)

G4A – Station Operation and setup

G4B – Test and monitoring equipment; two-tone test

G4C – Interference with consumer electronics; grounding; DSP

G4D – Speech processors; S meters; sideband operation near band edges

G4E – HF mobile radio installations; emergency and battery powered operation

Subelement G5 – Electrical principles

(3 Exam Questions – 3 Groups)

G5A – Reactance; inductance; capacitance; impedance; impedance matching

G5B – The Decibel; current and voltage dividers; electrical power calculations; sine wave root-mean-square (RMS) values; PEP calculations

G5C – Resistors; capacitors and inductors in series and parallel; transformers

Subelement G6 – Circuit components

(3 Exam Questions – 3 Groups)

G6A – Resistors; capacitors; inductors

G6B – Rectifiers; solid state diodes and transistors; vacuum tubes; batteries

G6C – Analog and digital integrated circuits (ICs); microprocessors; memory; I/O devices; microwave ICs (MMICs); display devices

Subelement G7 – Practical circuits

(3 Exam Questions – 3 Groups)

G7A – Power supplies; schematic symbols

G7B – Digital circuits; amplifiers and oscillators

G7C – Receivers and transmitters; filters, oscillators

Subelement G8 – Signals and emissions

(2 Exam Questions – 2 Groups)

G8A – Carriers and modulation; AM; FM; single and double sideband; modulation envelope; overmodulation

G8B – Frequency mixing; multiplication; HF data communications; bandwidths of various modes; deviation

Subelement G9 – Antennas and feed lines

(4 Exam Questions – 4 Groups)

G9A – Antenna feed lines; characteristic impedance and attenuation; SWR calculation, measurement and effects; matching networks

G9B – Basic antennas

G9C – Directional antennas

G9D – Specialized antennas

Subelement G0 – Electrical and RF safety

(2 Exam Questions – 2 Groups)

G0A – RF safety principles, rules and guidelines; routine station elevation

G0B – Safety in the ham shack; electrical shock and treatment, safety grounding, fusing, interlocks, wiring, antenna and tower safety

With a General license, you can use all VHF and UHF frequencies and most of the HF frequencies. You would have access to the 160, 30, 17, 12, and 10 meter bands and access to major parts of the 80, 40, 20, and 15 meter bands. Of course, this is in addition to all bands available to Technician license holders.

Amateur Extra is the third of three ham license classes. Like the Technician and General classes, you merely have to pass a test and pay your fee to get your Amateur Extra license. This class of license is more comprehensive than the lower license classes. The exam is longer – 50 questions – and the minimum passing score is higher – 37. However, once you get your Amateur Extra license, all ham frequencies, VHF, UHF and HF are available for your enjoyment. The Extra exam covers regulations, specialized operating practices, advanced electronics theory, and radio equipment design.

Like for the other license classes, the question pool for the Amateur Extra license is available online for downloading (http://www.ncvec.org/downloads/Final%202008%20Extra.pdf or http://www.ncvec.org/downloads/REVISED%202012-2016%20Extra%20Class%20Pool.doc). It is also available in print form in such publications as *The ARRL Extra Class License Manual Revised 9th Edition* (ISBN 978-0-87259-887-4). If you are downloading the question pool from the above web addresses, the first address is for the pool valid from July 1, 2008 until June 30, 2012. After July 1, 2012 (and until June 30, 2016) use the second address.

Topics for the Extra License in Amateur Radio (July 1, 2008 to June 30, 2012)

Below is the syllabus for the Amateur Extra Class for July 1, 2008 to June 30, 2012. (If you are going to take the Amateur Extra licensing exam after June 30, 2012, use the syllabus which follows this one.)

Subelement E1 — Commission's Rules

[6 Exam Questions – 6 Groups]

E1A – Operating Standards: frequency privileges for Extra Class amateurs; emission standards; automatic message forwarding; frequency sharing; FCC license actions; stations aboard ships or aircraft

E1B – Station restrictions and special operations: restrictions on station location; general operating restrictions, spurious emissions, control operator reimbursement; antenna structure restrictions; RACES operations

E1C – Station control: definitions and restrictions pertaining to local, automatic and remote control operation; control operator responsibilities for remote and automatically controlled stations

E1D – Amateur Satellite service: definitions and purpose; license requirements for space stations; available frequencies and bands; telecommand and telemetry operations; restrictions, and special provisions; notification requirements

E1E – Volunteer examiner program: definitions, qualifications, preparation and administration of exams; accreditation; question pools; documentation requirements

E1F – Miscellaneous rules: external RF power amplifiers; Line A; national quiet zone; business communications; compensated communications; spread spectrum; auxiliary stations; reciprocal operating privileges; IARP and CEPT licenses; third party communications with foreign countries; special temporary authority

---

Subelement E2 – Operating practices and procedures

[5 Exam Questions – 5 Groups]

E2A – Amateur radio in space: amateur satellites; orbital mechanics; frequencies and modes; satellite hardware; satellite operations

E2B – Television practices: fast scan television standards and techniques; slow scan television standards and techniques

E2C – Operating methods, part 1: contest and DX operating; spread-spectrum transmissions; automatic HF forwarding; selecting an operating frequency

E2D – Operating methods, part 2: VHF and UHF digital modes; packet clusters; Automatic Position Reporting System (APRS)

E2E – Operating methods, part 3: operating HF digital modes; error correction

---

Subelement E3 – Radio wave propagation

[3 Exam Questions – 3 Groups]

E3A – Propagation and technique, part 1: Earth-Moon-Earth communications; meteor scatter

E3B – Propagation and technique, part 2: transequatorial; long path; gray line; multi-path propagation

E3C – Propagation and technique, part 3: Auroral propagation; selective fading; radio-path horizon; take-off angle over flat or sloping terrain; earth effects on propagation; less common propagation modes

Subelement E4 -- Amateur radio technology and measurements

[5 Exam Questions – 5 Groups]

E4A – Test equipment: analog and digital instruments; spectrum and network analyzers, antenna analyzers; oscilloscopes; testing transistors; RF measurements

E4B – Measurement technique and limitations: instrument accuracy and performance limitations; probes; techniques to minimize errors; measurement of "Q"; instrument calibration

E4C – Receiver performance characteristics, part 1: phase noise, capture effect, noise floor, image rejection, MDS, signal-to-noise-ratio; selectivity

E4D – Receiver performance characteristics, part 2: blocking dynamic range, intermodulation and cross-modulation interference; 3rd order intercept; desensitization; preselection

E4E – Noise suppression: system noise; electrical appliance noise; line noise; locating noise sources; DSP noise reduction; noise blankers

Subelement E5 – Electrical principles

[4 Exam Questions – 4 Groups]

E5A – Resonance and Q: characteristics of resonant circuits: series and parallel resonance; Q; half-power bandwidth; phase relationships in reactive circuits

E5B – Time constants and phase relationships: R/L/C time constants: definition; time constants in RL and RC circuits; phase angle between voltage and current; phase angles of series and parallel circuits

E5C – Impedance plots and coordinate systems: plotting impedances in polar coordinates; rectangular coordinates

E5D – AC and RF energy in real circuits: skin effect; electrostatic and electromagnetic fields; reactive power; power factor; coordinate systems

Subelement E6 – Circuit components

[6 Exam Questions – 6 Groups]

E6A – Semiconductor materials and devices: semiconductor materials (germanium, silicon, P-type, N-type); transistor types: NPN, PNP, junction, power; field-effect transistors: enhancement mode; depletion mode; MOS; CMOS; N-channel; P-channel

E6B – Semiconductor diodes

E6C – Integrated circuits: TTL digital integrated circuits; CMOS digital integrated circuits; gates

E6D – Optical devices and toroids: vidicon and cathode-ray tube devices; charge-coupled devices (CCDs); liquid crystal displays (LCDs); toroids: permeability, core material, selecting, winding

E6E – Piezoelectric crystals and MMICS: quartz crystals (as used in oscillators and filters); monolithic amplifiers (MMICs)

E6F – Optical components and power systems: photoconductive principles and effects, photovoltaic systems, optical couplers, optical sensors, and optoisolators

Subelement E7 – Practical circuits

[8 Exam Questions – 8 Groups]

E7 – Digital circuits: digital circuit principles and logic circuits: classes of logic elements; positive and negative logic; frequency dividers; truth tables

E7B – Amplifiers: Class of operation; vacuum tube and solid-state circuits; distortion and intermodulation; spurious and parasitic suppression; microwave amplifiers

E7C – Filters and matching networks: filters and impedance matching networks: types of networks; types of filters; filter applications; filter characteristics; impedance matching; DSP filtering

E7D – Power supplies and voltage regulators

E7E – Modulation and demodulation: reactance, phase and balanced modulators; detectors; mixer stages; DSP modulation and demodulation; software defined radio systems

E7F – Frequency markers and counters: frequency divider circuits; frequency marker generators; frequency counters

E7G – Active filters and op-amps: active audio filters; characteristics; basic circuit design; operational amplifiers

E7H – Oscillators and signal sources: types of oscillators; synthesizers and phase-locked loops; direct digital synthesizers

Subelement E8 – Signals and emissions

[4 Exam Questions – 4 Groups]

E8A – AC waveforms: sine, square, sawtooth and irregular waveforms; AC measurements; average and PEP of RF signals; pulse and digital signal waveforms

E8B – Modulation and demodulation: modulation methods; modulation index and deviation ratio; pulse modulation; frequency and time division multiplexing

E8C – Digital signals: digital communications modes; CW; information rate vs. bandwidth; spread-spectrum communications; modulation methods

E8D – Waves, measurements, and RF grounding: peak-to-peak values, polarization; RF grounding

Subelement E9 – Antennas and transmission lines

[8 Exam Questions – 8 Groups]

E9A – Isotropic and gain antennas: definition; used as a standard for comparison; radiation pattern; basic antenna parameters: radiation resistance and reactance, gain, beamwidth, efficiency

E9B – Antenna patterns: E and H plane patterns; gain as a function of pattern; antenna design (computer modeling of antennas); Yagi antennas

E9C – Wire and phased vertical antennas: beverage antennas; terminated and resonant rhombic antennas; elevation above real ground; ground effects as related to polarization; take-off angles

E9D – Directional antennas: gain; satellite antennas; antenna beamwidth; losses; SWR bandwidth; antenna efficiency; shortened and mobile antennas; grounding

E9E – Matching: matching antennas to feed lines; power dividers

E9F – Transmission lines: characteristics of open and shorted feed lines: 1/8 wavelength; 1/4 wavelength; 1/2 wavelength; feed lines: coax versus open-wire; velocity factor; electrical length; transformation characteristics of line terminated in impedance not equal to characteristic impedance

E9G – The Smith chart

E9F

Subelement E0 – Safety

[1 exam question – 1 group]
E0A – Safety: amateur radio safety practices; RF radiation hazards; hazardous materials

Topics for the Extra License in Amateur Radio (July 1, 2012 to June 30, 2016)

Below is the syllabus for the Amateur Extra Class for July 1, 2012 to June 30, 2016. (If you are going to take the Amateur Extra exam prior to July 1, 2012, use the above syllabus.)

Subelement E1 – Commission's Rules

[6 Exam Questions – 6 Groups]
E1A – Operating Standards: frequency privileges; emission standards; automatic message forwarding; frequency sharing; stations aboard ships or aircraft

E1B – Station restrictions and special operations: restrictions on station location; general operating restrictions, spurious emissions, control operator reimbursement; antenna structure restrictions; RACES operations

E1C – Station control: definitions and restrictions pertaining to local, automatic and remote control operation; control operator responsibilities for remote and automatically controlled stations

E1D – Amateur Satellite service: definitions and purpose; license requirements for space stations; available frequencies and bands; telecommand and telemetry operations; restrictions, and special provisions; notification requirements

E1E – Volunteer examiner program: definitions, qualifications, preparation and administration of exams; accreditation; question pools; documentation requirements

E1F – Miscellaneous rules: external RF power amplifiers; national quiet zone; business communications; compensated communications; spread spectrum; auxiliary stations; reciprocal operating privileges; IARP and CEPT licenses; third party communications with foreign countries; special temporary authority

Subelement E2 – Operating procedures

[5 Exam Questions – 5 Groups]
E2A – Amateur radio in space: amateur satellites; orbital mechanics; frequencies and modes; satellite hardware; satellite operations

E2B – Television practices: fast scan television standards and techniques; slow scan television standards and techniques

E2C – Operating methods: contest and DX operating; spread-spectrum transmissions; selecting an operating frequency

E2D – Operating methods: VHF and UHF digital modes; APRS

E2E – Operating methods: operating HF digital modes; error correction

Subelement E3 – Radio wave propagation

[3 Exam Questions – 3 Groups]

E3A – Propagation and technique, Earth-Moon-Earth communications; meteor scatter

E3B – Propagation and technique, trans-equatorial; long path; gray-line; multi-path propagation

E3C – Propagation and technique, Aurora propagation; selective fading; radio-path horizon; take-off angle over flat or sloping terrain; effects of ground on propagation; less common propagation modes

Subelement E4 – Amateur practices

[5 Exam Questions – 5 Groups]

E4A – Test equipment: analog and digital instruments; spectrum and network analyzers, antenna analyzers; oscilloscopes; testing transistors; RF measurements

E4B – Measurement technique and limitations: instrument accuracy and performance limitations; probes; techniques to minimize errors; measurement of "Q"; instrument calibration

E4C – Receiver performance characteristics, phase noise, capture effect, noise floor, image rejection, MDS, signal-to-noise-ratio; selectivity

E4D – Receiver performance characteristics, blocking dynamic range, intermodulation and cross-modulation interference; 3rd order intercept; desensitization; preselection

E4E – Noise suppression: system noise; electrical appliance noise; line noise; locating noise sources; DSP noise reduction; noise blankers

Subelement E5 – Electrical principles

[4 Exam Questions – 4 Groups]

E5A – Resonance and Q: characteristics of resonant circuits: series and parallel resonance; Q; half-power bandwidth; phase relationships in reactive circuits

E5B – Time constants and phase relationships: RLC time constants: definition; time constants in RL and RC circuits; phase angle between voltage and current; phase angles of series and parallel circuits

E5C – Impedance plots and coordinate systems: plotting impedances in polar coordinates; rectangular coordinates

E5D – AC and RF energy in real circuits: skin effect; electrostatic and electromagnetic fields; reactive power; power factor; coordinate systems

Subelement E6 – Circuit components

[6 Exam Questions – 6 Groups]

E6A – Semiconductor materials and devices: semiconductor materials germanium, silicon, P-type, N-type; transistor types: NPN, PNP, junction, field-effect transistors: enhancement mode; depletion mode; MOS; CMOS; N-channel; P-channel

E6B – Semiconductor diodes

E6C – Integrated circuits: TTL digital integrated circuits; CMOS digital integrated circuits; gates

E6D – Optical devices and toroids: cathode-ray tube devices; charge-coupled devices (CCDs); liquid crystal displays (LCDs); toroids: permeability, core material, selecting, winding

E6E – Piezoelectric crystals and MMICs: quartz crystals; crystal oscillators and filters; monolithic amplifiers

E6F – Optical components and power systems: photoconductive principles and effects, photovoltaic systems, optical couplers, optical sensors, and optoisolators

Subelement E7 – Practical circuits

[8 Exam Questions – 8 Groups]

E7A – Digital circuits: digital circuit principles and logic circuits: classes of logic elements; positive and negative logic; frequency dividers; truth tables

E7B – Amplifiers: Class of operation; vacuum tube and solid-state circuits; distortion and intermodulation; spurious and parasitic suppression; microwave amplifiers

E7C – Filters and matching networks: filters and impedance matching networks: types of networks; types of filters; filter applications; filter characteristics; impedance matching; DSP filtering

E7D – Power supplies and voltage regulators

E7E – Modulation and demodulation: reactance, phase and balanced modulators; detectors; mixer stages; DSP modulation and demodulation; software defined radio systems

E7F – Frequency markers and counters: frequency divider circuits; frequency marker generators; frequency counters

E7G – Active filters and op-amps: active audio filters; characteristics; basic circuit design; operational amplifiers

E7H – Oscillators and signal sources: types of oscillators; synthesizers and phase-locked loops; direct digital synthesizers

Subelement E8 – Signals and emissions

[4 Exam Questions – 4 Groups]

E8A – AC waveforms: sine, square, sawtooth and irregular waveforms; AC measurements; average and PEP of RF signals; pulse and digital signal waveforms

E8B – Modulation and demodulation: modulation methods; modulation index and deviation ratio; pulse modulation; frequency and time division multiplexing

E8C – Digital signals: digital communications modes; CW; information rate vs. bandwidth; spread-spectrum communications; modulation methods

E8D – Waves, measurements, and RF grounding: peak-to-peak values, polarization; RF grounding

Subelement E9 – Antennas and transmission lines

[8 Exam Questions – 8 Groups]

E9A – Isotropic and gain antennas: definition; used as a standard for comparison; radiation pattern; basic antenna parameters: radiation resistance and reactance, gain, beamwidth, efficiency

E9B – Antenna patterns: E and H plane patterns; gain as a function of pattern; antenna design; Yagi antennas

E9C – Wire and phased vertical antennas: beverage antennas; terminated and resonant rhombic antennas; elevation above real ground; ground effects as related to polarization; take-off angles

E9D – Directional antennas: gain; satellite antennas; antenna beamwidth; losses; SWR bandwidth; antenna efficiency; shortened and mobile antennas; grounding

E9E – Matching: matching antennas to feed lines; power dividers

E9F – Transmission lines: characteristics of open and shorted feed lines: 1/8 wavelength; 1/4 wavelength; 1/2 wavelength; feed lines: coax versus open-wire; velocity factor; electrical length; transformation characteristics of line terminated in impedance not equal to characteristic impedance

E9G – The Smith chart

E9H – Effective radiated power; system gains and losses; radio direction finding antennas

Subelement E0 – Safety

[1 exam question – 1 group]

E0A – Safety: amateur radio safety practices; RF radiation hazards; hazardous materials

Once your new call sign is listed in the FCC database, you are good to go. For an Amateur Extra license in Texas, your call sign will consist of a prefix of K, N or W, the number five (5), and a two-letter suffix, or a two-letter prefix beginning with A, N, K or W, the number five (5), and a one-letter suffix, or a two-letter prefix beginning with A, the number four (4), and a two-letter suffix.

Ham radio equipment can be expensive or you can do it "on the cheap." The cost will run from a couple hundred dollars to well in the thousands, depending on what you have available. eBay, and Craigslist are good places to start looking. Most ham clubs do some sort of hamfest annually wherein club members or others are willing to part with older equipment. See Appendix A for a list of clubs in the Big Bend Region of Texas.

Another excellent source of equipment, as well as advice on setting the equipment up and how to use it properly, is current ham operators. In Appendix B, the author has listed all the FCC licensed ham operators in the Big Bend Region of Texas, listed by city, and then sorted by street and house number on the street. Who knows, maybe someone who lives close to you is a ham operator. Be a good neighbor, stop by and have a chat with him/her.

Like CB radios, ham radios come in three formats – base, mobile, and handheld. They can use the electric company for power, or operate off a car battery. In the opinion of this author, in spite of the slightly higher cost of the equipment and having to take a test to legally use the equipment, ham radio is the way to go when concerned about communication during times of crisis.

Canadian Call Sign Prefixes

Because of our proximity to Canada, many times ham contact is made with our northern neighbors. Below is a chart showing the origin of Canadian call sign prefixes.

Call Sign Prefix	Provence or Territory
CY0	Sable Island
CY9	St. Paul Island
VA1, VE1	New Brunswick, Nova Scotia
VA2, VE2	Quebec
VA3, VE3	Ontario
VA4, VE4	Manitoba
VA5, VE5	Saskatchewan
VA6, VE6	Alberta
VA7, VE7	British Columbia
VE8	North West Territories
VE9	New Brunswick
VO1	Newfoundland
VO2	Labrador
VY0	Nunavut
VY1	Yukon
VY2	Prince Edward Island

Common Radio Bands in the United States

Certain radio bands are more popular with ham radio enthusiasts than others. Below is a chart showing these bands and when they are most popular.

	Band (meter)	Frequency (MHz)	Use
HF	160	1.8 – 2.0	Night
	80	3.5 – 4.0	Night and Local Day
	40	7.0 – 7.3	Night and Local Day
	30	10.1 – 10.15	CW and Digital
	20	14.0 – 14.350	World Wide Day and Night
	17	18.068 – 18.168	World Wide Day and Night
	15	21.0 – 21.450	Primarily Daytime
	12	24.890 – 24.990	Primarily Daytime
	10	28.0 – 29.70	Daytime during Sunspot highs
VHF	6	50 – 54	Local to World Wide
	2	144 – 148	Local to Medium Distance
UHF	70 cm	430 – 440	Local

Common Amateur Radio Bands in Canada

160 Meter Band - Maximum bandwidth 6 kHz
1.800 - 1.820 MHz - CW
1.820 - 1.830 MHz - Digital Modes
1 830 - 1.840 MHz - DX Window
1.840 - 2.000 MHz - SSB and other wide band modes

80 Meter Band - Maximum bandwidth 6 kHz
3.500 - 3.580 MHz - CW
3.580 - 3.620 MHz - Digital Modes
3.620 - 3.635 MHz - Packet/Digital Secondary
3.635 - 3.725 MHz - CW
3.725 - 3.790 MHz - SSB and other side band modes*
3.790 - 3.800 MHz - SSB DX Window
3.800 - 4.000 MHz - SSB and other wide band modes

40 Meter Band - Maximum bandwidth 6 kHz
7.000 - 7.035 MHz - CW
7.035 - 7.050 MHz - Digital Modes
7.040 - 7.050 MHz - International packet
7.050 - 7.100 MHz - SSB
7.100 - 7.120 MHz - Packet within Region 2
7.120 - 7.150 MHz - CW
7.150 - 7.300 MHz - SSB and other wide band modes

30 Meter Band - Maximum bandwidth 1 kHz
10.100 - 10.130 MHz - CW only
10.130 - 10.140 MHz - Digital Modes
10.140 - 10.150 MHz - Packet

20 Meter Band - Maximum bandwidth 6 kHz
14.000 - 14.070 MHz - CW only
14.070 - 14.095 MHz - Digital Mode
14.095 - 14.099 MHz - Packet
14.100 MHz - Beacons
14.101 - 14.112 MHz - CW, SSB, packet shared
14.112 - 14.350 MHz - SSB
14.225 - 14.235 MHz - SSTV

17 Meter Band - Maximum bandwidth 6 kHz
18.068 - 18.100 MHz - CW
18.100 - 18.105 MHz - Digital Modes

18.105 - 18.110 MHz - Packet
18.110 - 18.168 MHz - SSB and other wide band modes

15 Meter Band - maximum bandwidth 6 kHz

21.000 - 21.070 MHz - CW
21.070 - 21.090 MHz - Digital Modes
21.090 - 21.125 MHz - Packet
21.100 - 21.150 MHz - CW and SSB
21.150 - 21.335 MHz - SSB and other wide band modes
21.335 - 21.345 MHz - SSTV
21.345 - 21.450 MHz - SSB and other wide band modes

12 Meter Band - Maximum bandwidth 6 kHz

24.890 - 24.930 MHz - CW
24.920 - 24.925 MHz - Digital Modes
24.925 - 24.930 MHz - Packet
24.930 - 24.990 MHz - SSB and other wide band modes

10 Meter Band - Maximum band width 20 kHz

28.000 - 28.200 MHz - CW
28.070 - 28.120 MHz - Digital Modes
28.120 - 28.190 MHz - Packet
28.190 - 28.200 MHz - Beacons
28.200 - 29.300 MHz - SSB and other wide band modes
29.300 - 29.510 MHz - Satellite
29.510 - 29.700 MHz - SSB, FM and repeaters

160 Meters (1.8-2.0 MHz)

1.800 - 2.000 CW
1.800 - 1.810 Digital Modes
1.810 CW QRP
1.843-2.000 SSB, SSTV and other wideband modes
1.910 SSB QRP
1.995 - 2.000 Experimental
1.999 - 2.000 Beacons

80 Meters (3.5-4.0 MHz)

3.590 RTTY/Data DX
3.570-3.600 RTTY/Data
3.790-3.800 DX window
3.845 SSTV
3.885 AM calling frequency

40 Meters (7.0-7.3 MHz)

7.040 RTTY/Data DX
7.080-7.125 RTTY/Data
7.171 SSTV
7.290 AM calling frequency

30 Meters (10.1-10.15 MHz)

10.130-10.140 RTTY
10.140-10.150 Packet

20 Meters (14.0-14.35 MHz)

14.070-14.095 RTTY
14.095-14.0995 Packet
14.100 NCDXF Beacons
14.1005-14.112 Packet
14.230 SSTV
14.286 AM calling frequency

17 Meters (18.068-18.168 MHz)

18.100-18.105 RTTY
18.105-18.110 Packet

15 Meters (21.0-21.45 MHz)

21.070-21.110 RTTY/Data
21.340 SSTV

12 Meters (24.89-24.99 MHz)

24.920-24.925 RTTY
24.925-24.930 Packet

10 Meters (28-29.7 MHz)

28.000-28.070 CW
28.070-28.150 RTTY
28.150-28.190 CW
28.200-28.300 Beacons
28.300-29.300 Phone
28.680 SSTV
29.000-29.200 AM
29.300-29.510 Satellite Downlinks
29.520-29.590 Repeater Inputs
29.600 FM Simplex
29.610-29.700 Repeater Outputs

6 Meters (50-54 MHz)

50.0-50.1 CW, beacons

50.060-50.080 beacon subband
50.1-50.3 SSB, CW
50.10-50.125 DX window
50.125 SSB calling
50.3-50.6 All modes
50.6-50.8 Nonvoice communications
50.62 Digital (packet) calling
50.8-51.0 Radio remote control (20-kHz channels)
51.0-51.1 Pacific DX window
51.12-51.48 Repeater inputs (19 channels)
51.12-51.18 Digital repeater inputs
51.5-51.6 Simplex (six channels)
51.62-51.98 Repeater outputs (19 channels)
51.62-51.68 Digital repeater outputs
52.0-52.48 Repeater inputs (except as noted; 23 channels)
52.02, 52.04 FM simplex
52.2 TEST PAIR (input)
52.5-52.98 Repeater output (except as noted; 23 channels)
52.525 Primary FM simplex
52.54 Secondary FM simplex
52.7 TEST PAIR (output)
53.0-53.48 Repeater inputs (except as noted; 19 channels)
53.0 Remote base FM simplex
53.02 Simplex
53.1, 53.2, 53.3, 53.4 Radio remote control
53.5-53.98 Repeater outputs (except as noted; 19 channels)
53.5, 53.6, 53.7, 53.8 Radio remote control
53.52, 53.9 Simplex

2 Meters (144-148 MHz)

144.00-144.05 EME (CW)
144.05-144.10 General CW and weak signals
144.10-144.20 EME and weak-signal SSB
144.200 National calling frequency
144.200-144.275 General SSB operation
144.275-144.300 Propagation beacons
144.30-144.50 New OSCAR subband
144.50-144.60 Linear translator inputs
144.60-144.90 FM repeater inputs
144.90-145.10 Weak signal and FM simplex (145.01,03,05,07,09 are widely used for packet)
145.10-145.20 Linear translator outputs
145.20-145.50 FM repeater outputs
145.50-145.80 Miscellaneous and experimental modes
145.80-146.00 OSCAR subband
146.01-146.37 Repeater inputs

146.40-146.58 Simplex
146.52 National Simplex Calling Frequency
146.61-146.97 Repeater outputs
147.00-147.39 Repeater outputs
147.42-147.57 Simplex
147.60-147.99 Repeater inputs

1.25 Meters (222-225 MHz)

222.0-222.150 Weak-signal modes
222.0-222.025 EME
222.05-222.06 Propagation beacons
222.1 SSB & CW calling frequency
222.10-222.15 Weak-signal CW & SSB
222.15-222.25 Local coordinator's option; weak signal, ACSB, repeater inputs, control
222.25-223.38 FM repeater inputs only
223.40-223.52 FM simplex
223.52-223.64 Digital, packet
223.64-223.70 Links, control
223.71-223.85 Local coordinator's option; FM simplex, packet, repeater outputs
223.85-224.98 Repeater outputs only

70 Centimeters (420-450 MHz)

420.00-426.00 ATV repeater or simplex with 421.25 MHz video carrier control links and experimental
426.00-432.00 ATV simplex with 427.250-MHz video carrier frequency
432.00-432.07 EME (Earth-Moon-Earth)
432.07-432.10 Weak-signal CW
432.10 70-cm calling frequency
432.10-432.30 Mixed-mode and weak-signal work
432.30-432.40 Propagation beacons
432.40-433.00 Mixed-mode and weak-signal work
433.00-435.00 Auxiliary/repeater links
435.00-438.00 Satellite only (internationally)
438.00-444.00 ATV repeater input with 439.250-MHz video carrier frequency and repeater links
442.00-445.00 Repeater inputs and outputs (local option)
445.00-447.00 Shared by auxiliary and control links, repeaters and simplex (local option)
446.00 National simplex frequency
447.00-450.00 Repeater inputs and outputs (local option)

33 Centimeters (902-928 MHz)

902.0-903.0 Narrow-bandwidth, weak-signal communications
902.0-902.8 SSTV, FAX, ACSSB, experimental
902.1 Weak-signal calling frequency
902.8-903.0 Reserved for EME, CW expansion
903.1 Alternate calling frequency
903.0-906.0 Digital communications

906-909 FM repeater inputs
909-915 ATV
915-918 Digital communications
918-921 FM repeater outputs
921-927 ATV
927-928 FM simplex and links

23 Centimeters (1240-1300 MHz)

1240-1246 ATV #1
1246-1248 Narrow-bandwidth FM point-to-point links and digital, duplex with 1258-1260.
1248-1258 Digital Communications
1252-1258 ATV #2
1258-1260 Narrow-bandwidth FM point-to-point links digital, duplexed with 1246-1252
1260-1270 Satellite uplinks, reference WARC '79
1260-1270 Wide-bandwidth experimental, simplex ATV
1270-1276 Repeater inputs, FM and linear, paired with 1282-1288, 239 pairs every 25 kHz, e.g. 1270.025, .050, etc.
1271-1283 Non-coordinated test pair
1276-1282 ATV #3
1282-1288 Repeater outputs, paired with 1270-1276
1288-1294 Wide-bandwidth experimental, simplex ATV
1294-1295 Narrow-bandwidth FM simplex services, 25-kHz channels
1294.5 National FM simplex calling frequency
1295-1297 Narrow bandwidth weak-signal communications (no FM)
1295.0-1295.8 SSTV, FAX, ACSSB, experimental
1295.8-1296.0 Reserved for EME, CW expansion
1296.00-1296.05 EME-exclusive
1296.07-1296.08 CW beacons
1296.1 CW, SSB calling frequency
1296.4-1296.6 Crossband linear translator input
1296.6-1296.8 Crossband linear translator output
1296.8-1297.0 Experimental beacons (exclusive)
1297-1300 Digital Communications

2300-2310 and 2390-2450 MHz

2300.0-2303.0 High-rate data
2303.0-2303.5 Packet
2303.5-2303.8 TTY packet
2303.9-2303.9 Packet, TTY, CW, EME
2303.9-2304.1 CW, EME
2304.1 Calling frequency
2304.1-2304.2 CW, EME, SSB
2304.2-2304.3 SSB, SSTV, FAX, Packet AM, Amtor
2304.30-2304.32 Propagation beacon network
2304.32-2304.40 General propagation beacons

2304.4-2304.5 SSB, SSTV, ACSSB, FAX, Packet AM, Amtor experimental
2304.5-2304.7 Crossband linear translator input
2304.7-2304.9 Crossband linear translator output
2304.9-2305.0 Experimental beacons
2305.0-2305.2 FM simplex (25 kHz spacing)
2305.20 FM simplex calling frequency
2305.2-2306.0 FM simplex (25 kHz spacing)
2306.0-2309.0 FM Repeaters (25 kHz) input
2309.0-2310.0 Control and auxiliary links
2390.0-2396.0 Fast-scan TV
2396.0-2399.0 High-rate data
2399.0-2399.5 Packet
2399.5-2400.0 Control and auxiliary links
2400.0-2403.0 Satellite
2403.0-2408.0 Satellite high-rate data
2408.0-2410.0 Satellite
2410.0-2413.0 FM repeaters (25 kHz) output
2413.0-2418.0 High-rate data
2418.0-2430.0 Fast-scan TV
2430.0-2433.0 Satellite
2433.0-2438.0 Satellite high-rate data
2438.0-2450.0 WB FM, FSTV, FMTV, SS experimental

3300-3500 MHz
3456.3-3456.4 Propagation beacons

5650-5925 MHz
5760.3-5760.4 Propagation beacons

10.00-10.50 GHz
10.368 Narrow band calling frequency 10.3683-10.3684 Propagation beacons
10.3640 Calling frequency

Now that you have your license (you do, don't you?), and your equipment, you are ready to go live. Below is a suggested start.

1) Assuming you have the HT set up to the appropriate frequency, and offset, press the mic button on the HT and say, "KK4HWX listening." Replace the KK4HWX with your own call sign, the one assigned to you by the FCC (it's the law). If no one responds to your call, you may wish to try again. Hopefully someone will respond to your call.

2) Once you get a response, it will be in the form of something like, "KK4HWX this is ??1??? in Eastport returning. My name is Florence. Back to you. ??1???" then a tone. Let us examine the response more closely. She first acknowledged your call sign

(KK4HWX), then identified hers (??1???). From the 1 in her call sign, you know that she first got her license in Region 1, meaning she got it while a resident of CT, ME, MA, NH, RI, or VT. She then told you where she's transmitting from (Eastport). The term "returning" means that she is returning your call. Her name is Florence. The phrase, "Back to you" indicates that she is turning over the conversation to you. She then repeats her call sign. The tone indicates to you that it is okay to proceed with your response. BTW if she had used the term "Over" instead of "Back to you," it would mean the same thing, just fewer words.

3) At this point, press the mic button and continue with the conversation. You should restate your call sign often during the conversation (perhaps every 10 minutes or less and whenever you begin transmitting). Don't forget to say, "Over" or "Back to you" whenever you are giving Florence control of the conversation again.

4) When you are ready to stop the conversation, you should say goodbye or use the phrase "73", meaning "best wishes." Your conversation would end something like, "??1??? 73, this is KK4HWX clear and monitoring." The "clear and monitoring" indicates that you are going to continue to monitor the frequency. If you are not going to continue monitoring, you may wish to end the conversation with Florence with, "clear and QRT" instead. The QRT means that you are stopping transmissions.

Call Sign Phonics

Because of different accents of various people, sometimes it is difficult to understand call sign letters when spoken. For this reason, most ham operators verbalize their call sign using phonics. Below is a table listing the accepted phonics for letters and numbers.

A = ALFA	S = SIERRA
B = BRAVO	T = TANGO
C = CHARLIE	U = UNIFORM
D = DELTA	V = VICTOR
E = ECHO	W = WHISKEY
F = FOXTROT	X = X-RAY
G = GOLF	Y = YANKEE
H = HOTEL	Z = ZULU (ZED)
I = INDIA	1 = ONE
J = JULIETT	2 = TWO
K = KILO	3 = THREE (TREE)
L = LIMA	4 = FOUR
M = MIKE	5 = FIVE (FIFE)
N = NOVEMBER	6 = SIX
O = OSCAR	7 = SEVEN
P = PAPA (PA-PA')	8 = EIGHT
Q = QUEBEC (KAY-BEK')	9 = NINE (NINER)
R = ROMEO	0 = ZERO

The words in parentheses are the pronunciation or the alternate pronunciations for the words or numbers, but you will hear both used. With the letter Z, (ZED) is by far the most commonly used. With the number 9, NINER is the most common and easiest to understand ON THE AIR.

If you wish to use Morse code (CW) instead of voice communication, the "conversation" would follow the same steps, with a few modifications. To type out each word would require a lot of typing and translating. If you are like this author, more means more, i.e., more typing means more typos are likely. To help with this situation, CW enthusiasts have developed a language all their own – they use abbreviations for common phrases. Below is a chart showing some of these abbreviations.

Abbreviation	Use
AR	Over
de	From or "this is"
ES	And
GM	Good Morning
K	Go
KN	Go only
NM	Name
QTH	Location
RPT	Report
R	Roger
SK	Clear
tnx	Thanks
UR	Your, you are
73	Best Wishes

Morse Code and Amateur Radio

If you wish to use CW, but are concerned about accuracy, you might consider purchasing a Morse code translator. This is an electronic device that you place in front of your speakers. It takes the CW sounds and translates them into English and displays the transmission on an LCD display. For the reverse, you can pick up a CW keyboard. With the keyboard, you type in your message and it converts the text to Morse code. The translator does not need to be attached to your ham equipment, whereas the keyboard would.

For your convenience, below is a table showing the Morse code signals and their meaning.

Character	Code
A	· —
B	— · · ·
C	— · — ·
D	— · ·

E	·
F	· · — ·
G	— — ·
H	· · · ·
I	· ·
J	· — — —
K	— · —
L	· — · ·
M	— —
N	— ·
O	— — —
P	· — — ·
Q	— — · —
R	· — ·
S	· · ·
T	—
U	· · —
V	· · · —
W	· — —
X	— · · —
Y	— · — —
Z	— — · ·
0	— — — — —
1	· — — — —
2	· · — — —
3	· · · — —
4	· · · · —
5	· · · · ·
6	— · · · ·
7	— — · · ·
8	— — — · ·
9	— — — — ·
Ampersand [&], Wait	· — · · ·
Apostrophe [']	· — — — — ·
At sign [@]	· — — · — ·
Colon [:]	— — — · · ·
Comma [,]	— — · · — —
Dollar sign [$]	· · · — · · —
Double dash [=]	— · · · —
Exclamation mark [!]	— · — · — —
Hyphen, Minus [-]	— · · · · —
Parenthesis closed [)]	— · — — · —
Parenthesis open [(]	— · — — ·
Period [.]	· — · — · —
Plus [+]	· — · — ·

27

Question mark [?]	· · — — · ·
Quotation mark ["]	· — · · — ·
Semicolon [;]	— · — · — ·
Slash [/], Fraction bar	— · · — ·
Underscore [_]	· · — — · —

An advantage of using Morse Code is that when broadcasting CW, you are using reduced power, thereby saving your battery. Your battery is used only while actually transmitting or receiving.

International Call Sign Prefixes

As was stated earlier, all ham radio call signs begin with letters (or numbers) taken from blocks assigned to each country of the world by the *ITU - International Telecommunications Union,* a body controlled by the United Nations. The following chart indicates which call sign series are allocated to which countries.

Call Sign Series	Allocated to
AAA-ALZ	**United States of America**
AMA-AOZ	Spain
APA-ASZ	Pakistan (Islamic Republic of)
ATA-AWZ	India (Republic of)
AXA-AXZ	Australia
AYA-AZZ	Argentine Republic
A2A-A2Z	Botswana (Republic of)
A3A-A3Z	Tonga (Kingdom of)
A4A-A4Z	Oman (Sultanate of)
A5A-A5Z	Bhutan (Kingdom of)
A6A-A6Z	United Arab Emirates
A7A-A7Z	Qatar (State of)
A8A-A8Z	Liberia (Republic of)
A9A-A9Z	Bahrain (State of)
BAA-BZZ	China (People's Republic of)
CAA-CEZ	Chile
CFA-CKZ	Canada
CLA-CMZ	Cuba
CNA-CNZ	Morocco (Kingdom of)
COA-COZ	Cuba
CPA-CPZ	Bolivia (Republic of)
CQA-CUZ	Portugal
CVA-CXZ	Uruguay (Eastern Republic of)
CYA-CZZ	Canada
C2A-C2Z	Nauru (Republic of)
C3A-C3Z	Andorra (Principality of)
C4A-C4Z	Cyprus (Republic of)

C5A-C5Z	Gambia (Republic of the)
C6A-C6Z	Bahamas (Commonwealth of the)
C7A-C7Z	World Meteorological Organization
C8A-C9Z	Mozambique (Republic of)
DAA-DRZ	Germany (Federal Republic of)
DSA-DTZ	Korea (Republic of)
DUA-DZZ	Philippines (Republic of the)
D2A-D3Z	Angola (Republic of)
D4A-D4Z	Cape Verde (Republic of)
D5A-D5Z	Liberia (Republic of)
D6A-D6Z	Comoros (Islamic Federal Republic of the)
D7A-D9Z	Korea (Republic of)
EAA-EHZ	Spain
EIA-EJZ	Ireland
EKA-EKZ	Armenia (Republic of)
ELA-ELZ	Liberia (Republic of)
EMA-EOZ	Ukraine
EPA-EQZ	Iran (Islamic Republic of)
ERA-ERZ	Moldova (Republic of)
ESA-ESZ	Estonia (Republic of)
ETA-ETZ	Ethiopia (Federal Democratic Republic of)
EUA-EWZ	Belarus (Republic of)
EXA-EXZ	Kyrgyz Republic
EYA-EYZ	Tajikistan (Republic of)
EZA-EZZ	Turkmenistan
E2A-E2Z	Thailand
E3A-E3Z	Eritrea
E4A-E4Z	Palestinian Authority
E5A-E5Z	New Zealand - Cook Islands (WRC-07)
E7A-E7Z	Bosnia and Herzegovina (Republic of) (WRC-07)
FAA-FZZ	France
GAA-GZZ	United Kingdom of Great Britain and Northern Ireland
HAA-HAZ	Hungary (Republic of)
HBA-HBZ	Switzerland (Confederation of)
HCA-HDZ	Ecuador
HEA-HEZ	Switzerland (Confederation of)
HFA-HFZ	Poland (Republic of)
HGA-HGZ	Hungary (Republic of)
HHA-HHZ	Haiti (Republic of)
HIA-HIZ	Dominican Republic
HJA-HKZ	Colombia (Republic of)
HLA-HLZ	Korea (Republic of)
HMA-HMZ	Democratic People's Republic of Korea
HNA-HNZ	Iraq (Republic of)
HOA-HPZ	Panama (Republic of)

HQA-HRZ	Honduras (Republic of)
HSA-HSZ	Thailand
HTA-HTZ	Nicaragua
HUA-HUZ	El Salvador (Republic of)
HVA-HVZ	Vatican City State
HWA-HYZ	France
HZA-HZZ	Saudi Arabia (Kingdom of)
H2A-H2Z	Cyprus (Republic of)
H3A-H3Z	Panama (Republic of)
H4A-H4Z	Solomon Islands
H6A-H7Z	Nicaragua
H8A-H9Z	Panama (Republic of)
IAA-IZZ	Italy
JAA-JSZ	Japan
JTA-JVZ	Mongolia
JWA-JXZ	Norway
JYA-JYZ	Jordan (Hashemite Kingdom of)
JZA-JZZ	Indonesia (Republic of)
J2A-J2Z	Djibouti (Republic of)
J3A-J3Z	Grenada
J4A-J4Z	Greece
J5A-J5Z	Guinea-Bissau (Republic of)
J6A-J6Z	Saint Lucia
J7A-J7Z	Dominica (Commonwealth of)
J8A-J8Z	Saint Vincent and the Grenadines
KAA-KZZ	**United States of America**
LAA-LNZ	Norway
LOA-LWZ	Argentine Republic
LXA-LXZ	Luxembourg
LYA-LYZ	Lithuania (Republic of)
LZA-LZZ	Bulgaria (Republic of)
L2A-L9Z	Argentine Republic
MAA-MZZ	United Kingdom of Great Britain and Northern Ireland
NAA-NZZ	**United States of America**
OAA-OCZ	Peru
ODA-ODZ	Lebanon
OEA-OEZ	Austria
OFA-OJZ	Finland
OKA-OLZ	Czech Republic
OMA-OMZ	Slovak Republic
ONA-OTZ	Belgium
OUA-OZZ	Denmark
PAA-PIZ	Netherlands (Kingdom of the)
PJA-PJZ	Netherlands (Kingdom of the) - Netherlands Antilles
PKA-POZ	Indonesia (Republic of)

PPA-PYZ	Brazil (Federative Republic of)
PZA-PZZ	Suriname (Republic of)
P2A-P2Z	Papua New Guinea
P3A-P3Z	Cyprus (Republic of)
P4A-P4Z	Netherlands (Kingdom of the) - Aruba
P5A-P9Z	Democratic People's Republic of Korea
RAA-RZZ	Russian Federation
SAA-SMZ	Sweden
SNA-SRZ	Poland (Republic of)
SSA-SSM	Egypt (Arab Republic of)
SSN-STZ	Sudan (Republic of the)
SUA-SUZ	Egypt (Arab Republic of)
SVA-SZZ	Greece
S2A-S3Z	Bangladesh (People's Republic of)
S5A-S5Z	Slovenia (Republic of)
S6A-S6Z	Singapore (Republic of)
S7A-S7Z	Seychelles (Republic of)
S8A-S8Z	South Africa (Republic of)
S9A-S9Z	Sao Tome and Principe (Democratic Republic of)
TAA-TCZ	Turkey
TDA-TDZ	Guatemala (Republic of)
TEA-TEZ	Costa Rica
TFA-TFZ	Iceland
TGA-TGZ	Guatemala (Republic of)
THA-THZ	France
TIA-TIZ	Costa Rica
TJA-TJZ	Cameroon (Republic of)
TKA-TKZ	France
TLA-TLZ	Central African Republic
TMA-TMZ	France
TNA-TNZ	Congo (Republic of the)
TOA-TQZ	France
TRA-TRZ	Gabonese Republic
TSA-TSZ	Tunisia
TTA-TTZ	Chad (Republic of)
TUA-TUZ	Côte d'Ivoire (Republic of)
TVA-TXZ	France
TYA-TYZ	Benin (Republic of)
TZA-TZZ	Mali (Republic of)
T2A-T2Z	Tuvalu
T3A-T3Z	Kiribati (Republic of)
T4A-T4Z	Cuba
T5A-T5Z	Somali Democratic Republic
T6A-T6Z	Afghanistan (Islamic State of)
T7A-T7Z	San Marino (Republic of)

T8A-T8Z	Palau (Republic of)
UAA-UIZ	Russian Federation
UJA-UMZ	Uzbekistan (Republic of)
UNA-UQZ	Kazakhstan (Republic of)
URA-UZZ	Ukraine
VAA-VGZ	Canada
VHA-VNZ	Australia
VOA-VOZ	Canada
VPA-VQZ	United Kingdom of Great Britain and Northern Ireland
VRA-VRZ	China (People's Republic of) - Hong Kong
VSA-VSZ	United Kingdom of Great Britain and Northern Ireland
VTA-VWZ	India (Republic of)
VXA-VYZ	Canada
VZA-VZZ	Australia
V2A-V2Z	Antigua and Barbuda
V3A-V3Z	Belize
V4A-V4Z	Saint Kitts and Nevis
V5A-V5Z	Namibia (Republic of)
V6A-V6Z	Micronesia (Federated States of)
V7A-V7Z	Marshall Islands (Republic of the)
V8A-V8Z	Brunei Darussalam
WAA-WZZ	**United States of America**
XAA-XIZ	Mexico
XJA-XOZ	Canada
XPA-XPZ	Denmark
XQA-XRZ	Chile
XSA-XSZ	China (People's Republic of)
XTA-XTZ	Burkina Faso
XUA-XUZ	Cambodia (Kingdom of)
XVA-XVZ	Viet Nam (Socialist Republic of)
XWA-XWZ	Lao People's Democratic Republic
XXA-XXZ	China (People's Republic of) - Macao (WRC-07)
XYA-XZZ	Myanmar (Union of)
YAA-YAZ	Afghanistan (Islamic State of)
YBA-YHZ	Indonesia (Republic of)
YIA-YIZ	Iraq (Republic of)
YJA-YJZ	Vanuatu (Republic of)
YKA-YKZ	Syrian Arab Republic
YLA-YLZ	Latvia (Republic of)
YMA-YMZ	Turkey
YNA-YNZ	Nicaragua
YOA-YRZ	Romania
YSA-YSZ	El Salvador (Republic of)
YTA-YUZ	Serbia (Republic of) (WRC-07)
YVA-YYZ	Venezuela (Republic of)

Y2A-Y9Z	Germany (Federal Republic of)
ZAA-ZAZ	Albania (Republic of)
ZBA-ZJZ	United Kingdom of Great Britain and Northern Ireland
ZKA-ZMZ	New Zealand
ZNA-ZOZ	United Kingdom of Great Britain and Northern Ireland
ZPA-ZPZ	Paraguay (Republic of)
ZQA-ZQZ	United Kingdom of Great Britain and Northern Ireland
ZRA-ZUZ	South Africa (Republic of)
ZVA-ZZZ	Brazil (Federative Republic of)
Z2A-Z2Z	Zimbabwe (Republic of)
Z3A-Z3Z	The Former Yugoslav Republic of Macedonia
2AA-2ZZ	United Kingdom of Great Britain and Northern Ireland
3AA-3AZ	Monaco (Principality of)
3BA-3BZ	Mauritius (Republic of)
3CA-3CZ	Equatorial Guinea (Republic of)
3DA-3DM	Swaziland (Kingdom of)
3DN-3DZ	Fiji (Republic of)
3EA-3FZ	Panama (Republic of)
3GA-3GZ	Chile
3HA-3UZ	China (People's Republic of)
3VA-3VZ	Tunisia
3WA-3WZ	Viet Nam (Socialist Republic of)
3XA-3XZ	Guinea (Republic of)
3YA-3YZ	Norway
3ZA-3ZZ	Poland (Republic of)
4AA-4CZ	Mexico
4DA-4IZ	Philippines (Republic of the)
4JA-4KZ	Azerbaijani Republic
4LA-4LZ	Georgia (Republic of)
4MA-4MZ	Venezuela (Republic of)
4OA-4OZ	Montenegro (Republic of) (WRC-07)
4PA-4SZ	Sri Lanka (Democratic Socialist Republic of)
4TA-4TZ	Peru
4UA-4UZ	United Nations
4VA-4VZ	Haiti (Republic of)
4WA-4WZ	Democratic Republic of Timor-Leste (WRC-03)
4XA-4XZ	Israel (State of)
4YA-4YZ	International Civil Aviation Organization
4ZA-4ZZ	Israel (State of)
5AA-5AZ	Libya (Socialist People's Libyan Arab Jamahiriya)
5BA-5BZ	Cyprus (Republic of)
5CA-5GZ	Morocco (Kingdom of)
5HA-5IZ	Tanzania (United Republic of)
5JA-5KZ	Colombia (Republic of)
5LA-5MZ	Liberia (Republic of)

5NA-5OZ	Nigeria (Federal Republic of)
5PA-5QZ	Denmark
5RA-5SZ	Madagascar (Republic of)
5TA-5TZ	Mauritania (Islamic Republic of)
5UA-5UZ	Niger (Republic of the)
5VA-5VZ	Togolese Republic
5WA-5WZ	Samoa (Independent State of)
5XA-5XZ	Uganda (Republic of)
5YA-5ZZ	Kenya (Republic of)
6AA-6BZ	Egypt (Arab Republic of)
6CA-6CZ	Syrian Arab Republic
6DA-6JZ	Mexico
6KA-6NZ	Korea (Republic of)
6OA-6OZ	Somali Democratic Republic
6PA-6SZ	Pakistan (Islamic Republic of)
6TA-6UZ	Sudan (Republic of the)
6VA-6WZ	Senegal (Republic of)
6XA-6XZ	Madagascar (Republic of)
6YA-6YZ	Jamaica
6ZA-6ZZ	Liberia (Republic of)
7AA-7IZ	Indonesia (Republic of)
7JA-7NZ	Japan
7OA-7OZ	Yemen (Republic of)
7PA-7PZ	Lesotho (Kingdom of)
7QA-7QZ	Malawi
7RA-7RZ	Algeria (People's Democratic Republic of)
7SA-7SZ	Sweden
7TA-7YZ	Algeria (People's Democratic Republic of)
7ZA-7ZZ	Saudi Arabia (Kingdom of)
8AA-8IZ	Indonesia (Republic of)
8JA-8NZ	Japan
8OA-8OZ	Botswana (Republic of)
8PA-8PZ	Barbados
8QA-8QZ	Maldives (Republic of)
8RA-8RZ	Guyana
8SA-8SZ	Sweden
8TA-8YZ	India (Republic of)
8ZA-8ZZ	Saudi Arabia (Kingdom of)
9AA-9AZ	Croatia (Republic of)
9BA-9DZ	Iran (Islamic Republic of)
9EA-9FZ	Ethiopia (Federal Democratic Republic of)
9GA-9GZ	Ghana
9HA-9HZ	Malta
9IA-9JZ	Zambia (Republic of)
9KA-9KZ	Kuwait (State of)

9LA-9LZ	Sierra Leone
9MA-9MZ	Malaysia
9NA-9NZ	Nepal
9OA-9TZ	Democratic Republic of the Congo
9UA-9UZ	Burundi (Republic of)
9VA-9VZ	Singapore (Republic of)
9WA-9WZ	Malaysia
9XA-9XZ	Rwandese Republic
9YA-9ZZ	Trinidad and Tobago

Third-Party Communications and Amateur Radio

If all of this information about ham radios is somewhat intimidating, do not despair. "You" can still use ham radios for communications without being a licensed operator. Yes, you do have to have a ham license in order to legally transmit by ham equipment (or be under the direct supervision of someone else who is licensed), but there is an alternative – third-party communication.

Third-party communications occur when a licensed operator sends either written or verbal messages on behalf of unlicensed persons or organizations. There are two "controls" on third-party communication.

First, the communication must be noncommercial and of a personal nature. Asking a ham operator to contact another ham operator located in an area just hit by tornados and, because of being without power, phones do not work in Grandma Sally's city so you can check up on her, is okay. Asking a ham to send a message out that you have an old Chevy for sale would not be okay.

Second, the message must be going to a permitted area. Transmitting from a US location to another US location is okay, but transmitting from the US to another country may not. Because third-party communications bypass a country's normal telephone and postal systems, many foreign governments forbid such communications. In order to transmit from one country to another, the other country must have signed a third-party agreement with the US. What follows is a list of those countries that do have third-party a communications agreement with the US.

V2	Antigua / Barbuda
LU	Argentina
VK	Australia
V3	Belize
CP	Bolivia
T9	Bosnia-Herzegovina
PY	Brazil
VE	Canada
CE	Chile
HK	Colombia

D6	Comoros (Federal Islamic Republic of)
TI	Costa Rica
CO	Cuba
HI	Dominican Republic
J7	Dominica
HC	Ecuador
YS	El Salvador
C5	Gambia, The
9G	Ghana
J3	Grenada
TG	Guatemala
8R	Guyana
HH	Haiti
HR	Honduras
4X	Israel
6Y	Jamaica
JY	Jordan
EL	Liberia
V7	Marshall Islands
XE	Mexico
V6	Micronesia, Federated States of
YN	Nicaragua
HP	Panama
ZP	Paraguay
OA	Peru
DU	Philippines
VR6	Pitcairn Island
V4	St. Christopher / Nevis
J6	St. Lucia
J8	St. Vincent and the Grenadines
9L	Sierra Leone
ZS	South Africa
3DA	Swaziland
9Y	Trinidad / Tobago
TA	Turkey
GB	United Kingdom
CX	Uruguay
YV	Venezuela
4U1ITUITU	Geneva
4U1VICVIC	Vienna

Remember, before TSHTF, keep your pantry well stocked, your powder dry, and your batteries fully charged. 73

APPENDIX A

American Radio Relay League

Affiliated Amateur Radio Clubs in

Texas

ARRL Affiliated Club:	**Key City Amateur Radio Club**
City:	Abilene, TX
Call Sign:	KC5OLO

ARRL Affiliated Club:	**Big Bend Amateur Radio Club**
City:	Alpine, TX
Call Sign:	AD5BB
Links:	http://www.bigbendarc.com/

ARRL Affiliated Club:	**Panhandle Amateur Radio Club**
City:	Amarillo, TX
Call Sign:	W5WX
Links:	www.orgsites.com/tx/w5wx

ARRL Affiliated Club:	**CQ Ingleside**
City:	Aransas Pass, TX
Call Sign:	KF5NJQ

ARRL Affiliated Club:	**Arlington Amateur Radio Club Inc.**
City:	Arlington, TX
Call Sign:	K5SLD
Links:	www.k5sld.org

ARRL Affiliated Club:	**Athens Amateur Radio Club Inc.**
City:	Athens, TX
Call Sign:	K5EPH
Links:	http://athensarc.org

ARRL Affiliated Club:	**Austin Amateur Radio Club Inc**
City:	Austin, TX
Call Sign:	W5KA
Links:	http://austinhams.org/

ARRL Affiliated Club:	**Central TX DX and Contest Club**
City:	Austin, TX
Call Sign:	W5CT
Links:	www.ctdxcc.org

ARRL Affiliated Club:	**Austin Amateur Radio Club Inc**
City:	Austin, TX
Call Sign:	W5KA
Links:	Travis County ARES, Austin Amateur Radio Club, Inc., http://austinhams.org/

ARRL Affiliated Club:	**Travis County React**
City:	Austin, TX
Call Sign:	K5TCR
Links:	http://www.texasreact.org/travis/

ARRL Affiliated Club:	**Roadrunners Microwave Group**
City:	Austin, TX
Call Sign:	K5RMG
Links:	http://www.k5rmg.org

ARRL Affiliated Club:	**Texas VHF-FM Society**
City:	Austin, TX
Call Sign:	W5OGZ
Links:	www.txvhffm.org

ARRL Affiliated Club:	**Tricounty Amateur Radio Club**
City:	Azle, TX
Call Sign:	WC5C
Links:	http://www.wc5c.org

ARRL Affiliated Club:	**Bedford Amateur Radio Club**
City:	Bedford, TX
Call Sign:	K5BED
Links:	http://www.bedfordarc.org

ARRL Affiliated Club:	**Central Texas Amateur Radio Club**
City:	Belton, TX
Call Sign:	W5AMK
Links:	www.ctarc.org

ARRL Affiliated Club:	**Kendall Amateur Radio Society**
City:	Boerne, TX
Call Sign:	KB5TX

ARRL Affiliated Club:	**Fannin County Amateur Radio Club**
City:	Bonham, TX
Call Sign:	K5FRC
Links:	http://k5frc.org

ARRL Affiliated Club:	**Northwest Texas Amateur Radio Club**
City:	Borger, TX
Call Sign:	WA5CSF
Links:	www.qsl.net/WA5CSF

ARRL Affiliated Club:	**Heart of Texas Ham Operators Group**
City:	Brady, TX
Call Sign:	WA5HOT
Links:	www.hothog.org

ARRL Affiliated Club:	**Brenham Amateur Radio Club**
City:	Brenham, TX
Call Sign:	W5AUM
Links:	http://www.alpha1.net/~w5aum

ARRL Affiliated Club:	**Bryan Amateur Radio Club**
City:	Bryan, TX
Call Sign:	W5BCS
Links:	http://www.bryanarc.org/

ARRL Affiliated Club:	**Metrocrest Amateur Radio Society**
City:	Carrollton, TX
Call Sign:	KB5A
Links:	http://www.kb5a.org

ARRL Affiliated Club:	**Medina County Amateur Radio Club**
City:	Castroville, TX
Call Sign:	KD5DX
Links:	www.mcarc.org

ARRL Affiliated Club:	**Sam Houston Amateur Radio Klub**
City:	Cleveland, TX
Call Sign:	AI5M
Links:	sharkclub.org

ARRL Affiliated Club:	**Saltgrass Link System**
City:	Clute, TX
Call Sign:	WB5UGT
Links:	www.saltgrasslinksystem.com

ARRL Affiliated Club:	**Big Country Amateur Radio Net**
City:	Clyde, TX
Call Sign:	K5BAR
Links:	http://bcarn.net

ARRL Affiliated Club:	**Texas A & M Amateur Radio Club**
City:	College Station, TX
Call Sign:	W5AC
Links:	http://w5ac.tamu.edu

ARRL Affiliated Club:	**Texas DX Society**
City:	Conroe, TX
Call Sign:	K5DX
Links:	http://www.tdxs.net
ARRL Affiliated Club:	**Coppell Amateur Communication Club**
City:	Coppell, TX
Call Sign:	KD5OEW
ARRL Affiliated Club:	**Corpus Christi Amateur Radio Club, Inc.**
City:	Corpus Christi, TX
Call Sign:	W5MS
Links:	www.w5ms.com
ARRL Affiliated Club:	**South TX Amateur Radio Club**
City:	Corpus Christi, TX
Call Sign:	N5CRP
Links:	www.n5crp.org
ARRL Affiliated Club:	**Houston County Amateur Radio Club**
City:	Crockett, TX
Call Sign:	WA5EC
Links:	www.WA5EC-HCARC.ORG
ARRL Special Service Club:	**Dallas Amateur Radio Club**
City:	Dallas, TX
Call Sign:	W5FC
Links:	www.w5fc.org
ARRL Affiliated Club:	**North Texas Contest Club**
City:	Dallas, TX
ARRL Affiliated Club:	**Texas Repeater System, Inc.**
City:	Dallas, TX
Call Sign:	W5TRS
Links:	www.texasrepeatersystem.org
ARRL Affiliated Club:	**Dallas County REACT Amateur Radio Club**
City:	Dallas, TX
Call Sign:	W5DCR
Links:	www.dallasreact.org
ARRL Affiliated Club:	**K5BSA AMATEUR RADIO SOCIETY**
City:	Dallas, TX
Call Sign:	K5BSA

ARRL Affiliated Club: **Denton County Amateur Radio Association**
City: Denton, TX
Call Sign: W5NGU
Links: http://www.dcara.net

ARRL Affiliated Club: **Patriot Amateur Radio Club**
City: Denton, TX
Call Sign: W5UTT

ARRL Affiliated Club: **Tarleton Area Amateur Radio Club**
City: Dublin, TX
Links: http://taarc.rebelwolf.com

ARRL Affiliated Club: **Southwest Dallas County Amateur Radio Club**
City: Duncanville, TX
Call Sign: W5AUY
Links: www.swdcarc.org

ARRL Affiliated Club: **West Texas Repeater Association**
City: El Paso, TX
Call Sign: K5ELP
Links: http://k5elp.com/

ARRL Affiliated Club: **El Paso Amateur Radio Club**
City: El Paso, TX
Call Sign: W5ES
Links: http://www.w5es.org or http://www.qsl.net/w5es

ARRL Special Service Club: **Sun City Amateur Radio Club**
City: El Paso, TX
Call Sign: K5WPH

ARRL Affiliated Club: **Rains Amateur Radio Association**
City: Emory, TX
Call Sign: W5ENT
Links: http://www.w5ent.org/

ARRL Affiliated Club: **Amateur Radio Euless**
City: Euless, TX
Call Sign: W5EUL
Links: http://www.w5eul.com

ARRL Affiliated Club: **Hays/Caldwell Amateur Radio Club**
City: Fentress, TX
Call Sign: KE5LOT
Links: http://www.hchams.org

ARRL Affiliated Club:	**Kilocycle Club Of Ft Worth**
City:	Fort Worth, TX
Call Sign:	W5SH
Links:	www.qsl.net/w5sh

ARRL Affiliated Club:	**North Texas WPX Amateur Radio Club**
City:	Garland, TX
Call Sign:	AJ5DX

ARRL Affiliated Club:	**Garland Amateur Radio Club**
City:	Garland, TX
Call Sign:	K5QHD
Links:	http://www.k5qhd.org

ARRL Affiliated Club:	**Sun City Amateur Radio Society (SCARS)**
City:	Georgetown, TX
Call Sign:	K5SCT
Links:	http://www.sctxcaorg/suncity/clubs-groups/sites/amradio/

ARRL Affiliated Club:	**Lone Star Amateur Radio Association**
City:	Georgetown, TX
Call Sign:	W5IN
Links:	lsara.org

ARRL Affiliated Club:	**Williamson County Amateur Radio Club**
City:	Georgetown, TX
Call Sign:	WC5T
Links:	http://www.wcarc.com

| ARRL Affiliated Club: | **Young County Amateur Radio Club** |
| City: | Graham, TX |

ARRL Affiliated Club:	**K2BSA Amateur Radio Association**
City:	Grapevine, TX
Call Sign:	K2BSA
Links:	http://www.k2bsa.net

ARRL Affiliated Club:	**Sabine Valley Amateur Radio Association**
City:	Greenville, TX
Call Sign:	K5GVL
Links:	www.k5gvl.org

ARRL Affiliated Club:	**Clay County Amateur Radio Club**
City:	Henrietta, TX
Call Sign:	KF5DFD
Links:	http://www.ka5wlr.com

ARRL Affiliated Club: **Houston Amateur Radio Club**
City: Houston, TX
Call Sign: W5DPA
Links: http://w5dpa.home.att.net

ARRL Affiliated Club: **Johnson Space Center Amateur Radio Club**
City: Houston, TX
Call Sign: W5RRR
Links: http://www.w5rrr.org

ARRL Affiliated Club: **Houston Amateur Mobile Society**
City: Houston, TX
Links: http://2meterhams.org

ARRL Affiliated Club: **Jake McClain Driver Memorial Amateur Radio Club**
City: Houston, TX
Call Sign: KC5WXA

ARRL Special Service Club: Northwest ARS
City: Houston, TX
Call Sign: W5NC
Links: http://www.w5nc.net

ARRL Affiliated Club: **Texas Repeater Council, Inc.**
City: Houston, TX
Call Sign: K5TRC

ARRL Special Service Club: Northwest Amateur Radio Club
City: Houston, TX
Call Sign: W5NC
Links: http://www.w5nc.net

ARRL Affiliated Club: **Texas Repeater Council, Inc.**
City: Houston, TX
Call Sign: K5TRC

ARRL Affiliated Club: **Walker County Amateur Radio Group**
City: Huntsville, TX
Call Sign: W5HVL

ARRL Affiliated Club: **Hurst Amateur Radio Club**
City: Hurst, TX
Call Sign: W5HRC
Links: http://harc.comuv.com/

ARRL Affiliated Club:	**Irving Amateur Radio Club Inc**
City:	Irving, TX
Call Sign:	WA5CKF
Links:	http://www.irvingarc.org

ARRL Affiliated Club:	**Lakes Area Amateur Radio Club**
City:	Jasper, TX
Call Sign:	W5JAS

ARRL Affiliated Club:	**Jersey Village Amateur Radio Club**
City:	Jersey Village, TX
Call Sign:	KE5RIC

ARRL Affiliated Club:	**Northwest High School Amateur Radio Club**
City:	Justin, TX
Call Sign:	NW5HS

ARRL Affiliated Club:	**Katy Amateur Radio Society**
City:	Katy, TX
Call Sign:	KT5TX
Links:	http://www.katyars.com

ARRL Affiliated Club:	**Kaufman County Amateur Radio Emergency System**
City:	Kaufman, TX
Call Sign:	KE5KBY
Links:	http://www.kaufman-ares.org

ARRL Affiliated Club:	**Stephen F Austin Radio Club**
City:	Kenney, TX
Call Sign:	W5SFA
Links:	http://www.w5sfa.org

ARRL Affiliated Club:	**Hill Country Amateur Radio Club**
City:	Kerrville, TX
Call Sign:	N5HR
Links:	http://www.kerrhams.org

ARRL Affiliated Club:	**Highland Lakes Amateur Radio Club**
City:	Kingsland, TX
Call Sign:	K5HLA
Links:	http://hlarc.org

ARRL Affiliated Club:	**TX Emergency Amateur Communicators**
City:	Kingwood, TX
Call Sign:	W5SI
Links:	www.teac.net
ARRL Affiliated Club:	**Big Thicket Amateur Radio Club**
City:	Kountze, TX
Call Sign:	N5BTC
ARRL Affiliated Club:	**Lampasas Middle School Youth Amateur Radio Club**
City:	Lampasas, TX
Call Sign:	K5LMS
ARRL Affiliated Club:	**Laredo Hams Amateur Radio Club, Inc.**
City:	Laredo, TX
Call Sign:	W5LRD
Links:	www.LaredoHams.com
ARRL Affiliated Club:	**DX Contest Club**
City:	Leonard, TX
Call Sign:	KW5DX
ARRL Affiliated Club:	**Hockley County Amateur Radio Club**
City:	Levelland, TX
Call Sign:	WB5EMR
ARRL Affiliated Club:	**Longview East Texas Amateur Radio Club**
City:	Longview, TX
Call Sign:	KI5UA
ARRL Affiliated Club:	**Amateur Radio Society At Tech (TTU)**
City:	Lubbock, TX
Call Sign:	K5TTU
Links:	www.facebook.com/k5ttu, www.orgs.ttu.edu/arsat
ARRL Affiliated Club:	**Deep East Texas Amateur Radio Club, Inc.**
City:	Lufkin, TX
Call Sign:	W5IRP
Links:	www.detarc.net
ARRL Affiliated Club:	**Marshall Amateur Radio Club**
City:	Marshall, TX
Call Sign:	KB5MAR
Links:	www.marclub.net

ARRL Special Service Club: **Mc Kinney Amateur Radio Club**
City: Mc Kinney, TX
Call Sign: W5MRC
Links: http://www.mckinneyarc.org

ARRL Affiliated Club: **North Texas Homeschoolers Amateur Radio Club**
City: Melissa, TX
Call Sign: NT5HS
Links: http://www.qsl.net/nt5hs/

ARRL Affiliated Club: **Mc Kinney Emergency Repeater Association**
City: Melissa, TX
Call Sign: W5MRA

ARRL Special Service Club: **Ham Association of Mesquite**
City: Mesquite, TX
Call Sign: WJ5J
Links: http://www.wj5j.org

ARRL Special Service Club: **Midland Amateur Radio Club**
City: Midland, TX
Call Sign: W5QGG
Links: www.w5qgg.org

ARRL Affiliated Club: **Nacogdoches Amateur Radio Club**
City: Nacogdoches, TX
Call Sign: W5NAC
Links: http://www.w5nac.com

ARRL Affiliated Club: **Nacogdoches County Emergency Communications**
City: Nacogdoches, TX

ARRL Affiliated Club: **Jefferson County Amateur Radio Club**
City: Nederland, TX
Call Sign: W5SSV
Links: www.qsl.net/w5ssv, http://w5ssv.com

ARRL Affiliated Club: **Guadalupe Valley Amateur Radio Club**
City: New Braunfels, TX
Call Sign: WB5LVI
Links: http://groups.yahoo.com/group/gvarcllc/

ARRL Affiliated Club:	**North Richland Hills Amateur Radio Club**
City:	North Richland Hills, TX
Links:	http://www.nrharc.org

ARRL Affiliated Club:	**West Texas Amateur Radio Club**
City:	Odessa, TX
Call Sign:	WT5ARC
Links:	http://www.wtarc.org

ARRL Affiliated Club:	**Orange Amateur Radio Club Inc**
City:	Orange, TX
Call Sign:	W5ND
Links:	http://www.qsl.net/w5nd/

ARRL Affiliated Club:	**Palestine/Anderson County Amateur Radio Club**
City:	Palestine, TX
Call Sign:	K5PAL
Links:	http://www.pacarc.org

ARRL Affiliated Club:	**Red River Valley Amateur Radio Club**
City:	Paris, TX
Call Sign:	WB5RDD
Links:	http://www.wb5rdd.org

ARRL Affiliated Club:	**Northeast TX Radio Operations & Command, Inc.**
City:	Paris, TX
Call Sign:	WN5ROC

ARRL Affiliated Club:	**Pearland Amateur Radio Club**
City:	Pearland, TX
Call Sign:	K5PLD
Links:	http://www.k5pld.org

ARRL Affiliated Club:	**DFW Contest Group**
City:	Plano, TX
Links:	http://www.dfwcontest.com

ARRL Affiliated Club:	**Plano Amateur Radio Klub Inc.**
City:	Plano, TX
Call Sign:	K5PRK
Links:	www.k5prk.net

ARRL Affiliated Club:	**Atascosa County Amateur Radio Club**
City:	Pleasanton, TX
Call Sign:	WA5AR
Links:	www.wa5ar.org

ARRL Affiliated Club:	**Port Lavaca Amateur Radio Club**
City:	Port Lavaca, TX
Call Sign:	W5KTC
Links:	www.w5ktc.org

ARRL Affiliated Club:	**Buena Serta El Radio Society**
City:	Putnam, TX

ARRL Affiliated Club:	**Ransom Canyon Amateur Radio Club**
City:	Ransom Canyon, TX
Call Sign:	W5LCC
Links:	http://www.w5lcc.net

ARRL Affiliated Club:	**Rockwell-Collins Amateur Radio Club**
City:	Richardson, TX
Call Sign:	W5ROK
Links:	http://w5rok.us

ARRL Affiliated Club:	**Richardson Wireless Klub**
City:	Richardson, TX
Call Sign:	K5RWK
Links:	www.k5rwk.org

ARRL Affiliated Club:	**Rockwall Amateur Radio Club**
City:	Rockwall, TX
Call Sign:	K5RKW
Links:	www.rockwall-arc.org

ARRL Affiliated Club:	**Rowlett Amateur Radio Club**
City:	Rowlett, TX
Call Sign:	AD5WP
Links:	www.rowlettradio.com

ARRL Affiliated Club:	**Sachse Amateur Radio Association**
City:	Sachse, TX
Call Sign:	KF5NBO
Links:	http://www.sachseradio.org

ARRL Special Service Club:	**San Angelo Amateur Radio Club**
City:	San Angelo, TX
Call Sign:	W5QX
Links:	http://www.w5qx.org

ARRL Affiliated Club:	**San Antonio Radio Club**
City:	San Antonio, TX
Call Sign:	W5SC
Links:	http://www.w5sc.org

ARRL Affiliated Club:	**South Texas DX and Contest Club**
City:	San Antonio, TX
Call Sign:	W5RTA
Links:	www.stxdxcc.org

ARRL Affiliated Club:	**Intertie, Inc.**
City:	San Antonio, TX
Call Sign:	WX5II
Links:	http://www.intertie.org

ARRL Affiliated Club:	**San Benito Amateur Radio Club**
City:	San Benito, TX
Call Sign:	N5LNS

ARRL Affiliated Club:	**North Texas Microwave Society**
City:	Sanger, TX
Call Sign:	W5HN
Links:	http://www.ntms.org/

ARRL Affiliated Club:	**MARAC, Inc.**
City:	Santa Rosa, TX
Call Sign:	K9DCJ
Links:	http://marac.org

ARRL Affiliated Club:	**Chaparral Amateur Radio Club**
City:	Seguin, TX
Call Sign:	WA5GC

ARRL Affiliated Club:	**Grayson County Amateur Radio Club**
City:	Sherman, TX
Call Sign:	K5GCC
Links:	http://www.K5GCC.us

ARRL Affiliated Club:	**Bastrop County Amateur Radio Club**
City:	Smithville, TX
Call Sign:	KE5FKS
Links:	www.repeater.org/austinhams/bcarc/index.html

ARRL Affiliated Club:	**Northeast Tarrant Amateur Radio Club**
City:	Southlake, TX
Call Sign:	N5EOC
Links:	www.netarc.us

ARRL Affiliated Club:	**The Woodlands Emergency Communications Group**
City:	Spring, TX
Call Sign:	W5WFD
Links:	www.twarc.org

ARRL Affiliated Club:	**Brazos Valley Amateur Radio Club Inc**
City:	Sugar Land, TX
Call Sign:	KK5W
Links:	http://www.bvarc.com

ARRL Affiliated Club:	**South Texas Repeater Club**
City:	Sugar Land, TX
Links:	www.w5acm.net/stxrc.html

ARRL Affiliated Club:	**Hopkins County Amateur Radio Club**
City:	Sulphur Springs, TX
Call Sign:	K5SST
Links:	http://www.k5sst.org/

ARRL Affiliated Club:	**Temple Amateur Radio Club Inc.**
City:	Temple, TX
Call Sign:	W5LM
Links:	http://www.tarc.org

ARRL Affiliated Club:	**Tidelands Amateur Radio Society, Inc.**
City:	Texas City, TX
Call Sign:	K5BS
Links:	http://www.tidelands.org

Affiliated Club:	**Lake Area Amateur Radio Klub**
City:	The Colony, TX
Call Sign:	K5LRK
Links:	http://www.laark.net

ARRL Affiliated Club:	**Tyler Amateur Radio Club, Inc.**
City:	Tyler, TX
Call Sign:	K5TYR
Links:	http://tylerarc.org

ARRL Affiliated Club:	**Victoria Amateur Radio Club**
City:	Victoria, TX
Call Sign:	W5DSC
Links:	http://www.varc.us

ARRL Affiliated Club:	**Heart O' Texas Amateur Radio Club Inc**
City:	Waco, TX
Call Sign:	W5ZDN
Links:	http://hotarc.org

ARRL Affiliated Club:	**Heart of Texas DX Society**
City:	Waco, TX
Call Sign:	W5DXS
Links:	http://w5dxs.tripod.com/index.html

ARRL Affiliated Club:	**Ellis County Amateur Radio Club**
City:	Waxahachie, TX
Call Sign:	WD5DDH
Links:	http://www.wd5ddh.org

ARRL Special Service Club:	**Amateur Radio Club of Parker County, TX**
City:	Weatherford, TX
Call Sign:	W5PC
Links:	http://www.w5pc.org

ARRL Affiliated Club:	**Clear Lake Amateur Radio Club**
City:	Webster, TX
Call Sign:	K5HOU
Links:	http://www.clarc.org

ARRL Affiliated Club:	**Wichita Amateur Radio Society**
City:	Wichita Falls, TX
Call Sign:	N5WF
Links:	http://www.n5wf.org

ARRL Affiliated Club:	**Coleto Creek Amateur Radio Club**
City:	Yorktown, TX
Call Sign:	W5DWT
Links:	www.ccarc.us

APPENDIX B

Amateur Radio License Holders

in

Texas: Big Bend Region
(by City)

KC5YHS
Bobby D Goains
101 Acacia Trl
Alpine TX 79830

AB5OS
Bette H Adair
HC 65 Box 14B
Alpine TX 79830

AG4O
Roger W Adair
HC 65 Box 14B
Alpine TX 79830

KM5VM
Barbara N Stone
HC 65 Box 14G
Alpine TX 79830

WO5K
Robert M Mc Daniel
Box 1627
Alpine TX 79831

WA3GTU
Domenick S Murabito
HC65 Box 39D
Alpine TX 79830

KB5RKR
Eva K Duncan
Box 867
Alpine TX 79831

KB5YVK
Tennessee
Box 944
Alpine TX 79831

KE5IYO
Keith L Sternes
401 Cottonwood Creek Rd
Alpine TX 79830

KD7JYD
Urban W Strachan
205 East Ave B
Alpine TX 79830

KD5EIT

John L Sanders
609 East Ave E
Alpine TX 79830

W5WWX
Leslie Spoonts Jr
700 East Hancock Ave
Alpine TX 79830

KD5VYG
Anthony R Delacerda
306 East Harriett
Alpine TX 79830

N5DO
David L Cockrum
501 East June
Alpine TX 79830

KE5SYK
Richard G Gatewood
509 East June
Alpine TX 79830

KE5SYB
Forrest W Gatewood
509 East June St
Alpine TX 79830

W5MWX
August Koenig
2005 Enfield
Alpine TX 79831

N5SWW
Susan G Penney
2100 Fort Davis Hwy 1D
Alpine TX 79830

WA5MHO
A Dean Snedecor
6 Gray Addition
Alpine TX 79830

KB7ZWY
Britt Steele
24 Gray Addition
Alpine TX 79830

W5ATO
William R Baker
1200 Jeremy
Alpine TX 79830

N5SWU
Patricia Koch
400 Mosley Ln
Alpine TX 79830

N5WYH
Billy L Quarles
501 North 11th
Alpine TX 79831

N5JOE
Jim C Thomas
1206 North 4th St
Alpine TX 79830

W5QDH
William H Perryman
1005 North 5th
Alpine TX 79831

N5MVQ
Kaaren M Florstedt
1308 North 5th
Alpine TX 79830

AD5BB
Big Bend Amateur Radio Club
301 North 5th St
Alpine TX 79830

KE5YHV
Big Bend Amateur Radio Club
301 North 5th St
Alpine TX 79830

WA5ROE
Bobby C Ward
1402 North 5th St
Alpine TX 798302512

KD5TXK
John B Rayburn
907 North 6th St
Alpine TX 79830

KD5RLX
Joe I Ybarra Jr
1105 North 8th
Alpine TX 79830

KA5PVB
Charles A Dobbins
616 North Cherry St
Alpine TX 79830

KB5R
Walter E Herman III
2 Rim Rd
Alpine TX 79830

K5EIE
Maxwell G Moon
206 South 10th St
Alpine TX 798311624

KD5ESB
Albert R Lujan
405 South 14th
Alpine TX 79830

KD5QEC
Keith R West
905A South Harrison St
Alpine TX 79830

AD5JZ
Stephen F Neubauer
46561 State Hwy 118
Alpine TX 79830

W5RNJ
Elenor M Neubauer
46561 State Hwy 118
Alpine TX 79830

W5YT
Herbert Smith
2001 State Hwy 118 Apt 15
Alpine TX 79830

KP4FF
Steven H Posner
31 Sunny Glen
Alpine TX 79830

NF5FF
Steven H Posner
31 Sunny Glen
Alpine TX 79830

KD5SKX
Billy D Roberts
34 Sunny Glen
Alpine TX 79830

W5NPR
Billy D Roberts
34 Sunny Glen

Alpine TX 79830

KB2VUL
Charles O Neill
301 Tarantula Ranch Rd
Alpine TX 79830

WB5WYF
James B Seaman
 Terlingua Rt Box 247
Alpine TX 79830

N5NYZ
Thomas E Gius
206 West Arcadia
Alpine TX 79830

KF5IR
Douglas A Mc Guire
906 West Ave C
Alpine TX 79830

KD5GAN
Burke Headrick
702 West Eagle Pass
Alpine TX 79830

KD5VYF
Francisco A Garcia
308 West Fort Davis
Alpine TX 79830

K5FD
James E Cook
609 West Holland
Alpine TX 79830

KC5UWZ
Cecil R Milder
1008 West Marfa
Alpine TX 79830

WR7X
Burns M Landrum
2001 West Mosely Lp Box 12
Alpine TX 79830

KD5QEB
Thomas J Werneking
602 West Sanderson
Alpine TX 79830

WB5EGQ
John P White Jr

1104 West Sanderson Ave
Alpine TX 79830

KC5AEV
Linda J Martin
103 West Stockton
Alpine TX 79830

KF5KMA
Daniel M Walker
2001 West Sul Ross Ave
Alpine TX 79830

KE5KNQ
Robert J Kinucan
305 West Uvalde Ave
Alpine TX 79830

KA1AAJ
Robert A Ayer
807 West Uvalde St
Alpine TX 79830

KA1BJN
Claire Ayer
807 West Uvalde St
Alpine TX 79830

KE5OG
William L Brooks
Alpine TX 79830

K5AHI
Robert H Mastin
Alpine TX 79831

KC5ASH
Robbie M Ferguson
Alpine TX 79831

KD5MXR
Jose L Iniguez
Alpine TX 79831

KD5RJE
Lora L Hawkins
Alpine TX 79831

KD5SKY
Jonas K Edwards
Alpine TX 79831

KE5YCW
Margaret H Mattison

Alpine TX 79831

KE5YFD
James B Glasscock
Alpine TX 79831

KF5ESZ
George D Mattison
Alpine TX 79831

KF5HBQ
George D Mattison
Alpine TX 79831

KF5KMB
Polly K Mastin
Alpine TX 79831

N5MHN
Hope Teeples
Alpine TX 79831

N5QIA
Ken M Clouse Jr
Alpine TX 79831

N5SWV
Eve Trook White
Alpine TX 79831

W5DWI
Richard L Hawkins
Alpine TX 79831

W5GDM
George D Mattison
Alpine TX 79831

W5JUW
Lora L Hawkins
Alpine TX 79831

W5PKW
Jack W Scott
Alpine TX 79831

WA5JBG
James B Glasscock
Alpine TX 79831

WT5O
P Bert Teeples
Alpine TX 79831

KA0UGM
Vicki R Friddell
Alpine TX 798311230

N0FTL
William T Friddell
Alpine TX 798311230

W1BCN
Edward A J Gosselin
Alpine TX 79830

KB5GWC
Robert M Caughman
Alpine TX 79831

KB5RTM
Robert L Mc Graw III
Alpine TX 79831

KP2S
Dunn J Sibley III
Alpine TX 79831

N5SBV
Frank E Schretter
Alpine TX 79831

N5SWO
Charles W Cluck
Alpine TX 79831

FCC Amateur Radio Licenses in Anthony

KC1AL
Paul A Le Veille
601 Celeste St
Anthony TX 79821

N5ZRF
Denny R Clayton
709 Eduardo St
Anthony TX 798215108

N5XRO
Douglas T Frame
 SR Box 356
Anthony TX 79821

KA5ZJZ
Troy O Webb
Anthony TX 79821

FCC Amateur Radio Licenses in Balmorhea

W4LCC
Charles E Towry
 Box 254
Balmorhea TX 79718

KD5FYO
Ruben L Carrasco
Rt 1 Box 281
Balmorhea TX 79718

FCC Amateur Radio Licenses in Barstow

WB5AKC
Ernest T Travland
 Box 71
Barstow TX 79719

FCC Amateur Radio Licenses in Big Bend National Park

KC5JHF
Richard H Spens
Big Bend National Park TX 79834

FCC Amateur Radio Licenses in Canutillo

KE5EZW
Melissa A Orrantia
6744 1st St
Canutillo TX 79835

N5UXZ
Royce L Gatlin
7313 Branding Iron
Canutillo TX 79835

N5XYA
Randy L Gatlin
7313 Branding Iron Dr
Canutillo TX 79835

KB5SQB
Richard E Lazarin
913 Fairlane Dr
Canutillo TX 798358434

KE5YAI

Erick M Munoz
8713 Kingsway Dr
Canutillo TX 79835

KC5MRM
Carleton Talbot
140 Libby St
Canutillo TX 79835

KE5LGS
Jamelle K Taylor
7148 Statesburg -D
Canutillo TX 79835

W5AAM
Anthony A Mc Lean
500 Talbot Ave C 1
Canutillo TX 79835

KA5TWO
Jo Ann Faulk
Canutillo TX 79835

KA5OXC
Robert H Moses
Canutillo TX 798353011

KC5ZOQ
Arthur H Messer Jr
20045 4th St
Christoval TX 76935

N5YQK
James B Gilbreath
22326 Chula Vista
Christoval TX 769350343

WD5BTN
Leonard F Isaacs
1609 FM Rd 2084
Christoval TX 76935

K5EP
Grady P Blount
5790 Green Oaks Dr
Christoval TX 76935

KB5MP
Grady P Blount
5790 Green Oaks Dr
Christoval TX 76935

KC5ILD
Joe B Kent
3466 Leal Rd
Christoval TX 76935

KC5KXY
La Rae J Kent
3466 Leal Rd
Christoval TX 76935

W5JBK
Joe B Kent
3466 Leal Rd
Christoval TX 76935

W5UI
Joe B Kent
3466 Leal Rd
Christoval TX 76935

KF5EFV
George Broughton
5454 Scenic Bluff Trl
Christoval TX 76935

W5DAB
David A Bell
3030 Venado Dr
Christoval TX 76935

N5ZSO
Wempford R Williams
3406 Venado Rd
Christoval TX 76935

KD5URV
James L Cleveland
Christoval TX 76935

KE5TXA
Eva J Mullen
Christoval TX 76935

KE5YHJ
Bryce Dupree
Christoval TX 76935

N5DRF
Barbara S Herring
Box 95

Clint TX 79836

K5JGB
Jimmie G Britton Jr
Clint TX 79836

KD5PC
Russell D Herring
Clint TX 79836

KE5IJF
Jimmie G Britton Jr
Clint TX 79836

WA5MFI
Roderick E Britton
Clint TX 79836

KB5HUK
Alonzo Rodriguez
Clint TX 79836

KD5SEO
David J Kelley
Comstock TX 78837

KE5LOU
David S Rice
Comstock TX 78837

KE5MKQ
Christopher A Villegas
2305 Brook Dr
Crane TX 79731

KE5MKY
William S Woody
1101 South Virginia
Crane TX 79731

WB5WYI
William C Pearson
304 Virginia
Crane TX 79731

KB5PQE
Robert L Van Vickle Jr
 Hamilton Ln
Del Rio TX 78840

W5PUF
Richard W Spencer
155 Agua Serena
Del Rio TX 78840

W5DRS
Donald E Arnold
111 Alambre Dr
Del Rio TX 78840

KE5TDH
Debra L Todd
124 Alta Vista
Del Rio TX 78840

N5MQX
Gary E Martin
126 Alta Vista
Del Rio TX 78840

KF5XY
Keith A Steffey
100 Alta Vista Dr
Del Rio TX 78840

KC5VCZ
Lloyd D Johnson
409 Anchor St
Del Rio TX 788403396

N5YUQ
Ruben A De Los Santos
112 Angela Dr
Del Rio TX 78840

KB5QIR
Elizabeth Gomez
1402 Ave A
Del Rio TX 78840

K5CDL
Charles D Lynde
1804 Ave C
Del Rio TX 78840

N5YUS
Enriqueta L Bermea
601 Ave G
Del Rio TX 78840

KB5QIS
Sergio A Leon
1406 Ave P
Del Rio TX 78840

KB5QJU
Richard Roman
1700 Ave P
Del Rio TX 78840

KB5QIU
Johnny Vargas III
1801 Ave Q
Del Rio TX 78840

KB5YVV
James E Miller
HCR 2 Box 151
Del Rio TX 78840

KE5IHI
Timothy A Mitchell
HCR 1 Box 29
Del Rio TX 78840

KB5PQQ
Daniel Aguero
HCR 2 Box 37F
Del Rio TX 78840

KC9AJ
Frank W Denk Sr
Hrc 3 Box 41M Hwy 90W
Del Rio TX 78840

N5PQW
Tammy L Sorensen
HCR 3 Box 43North Hwy 90W
Del Rio TX 78840

KE5QIV
James D Powers
HCR 3 Box 4B Hitching Post
Rd
Del Rio TX 78840

KC5FOA
Francisco J Aguero
HCR 2 Box 82
Del Rio TX 78840

KD5YAL
Vincente Rodriguez Jr

HCR 3 Box Y
Del Rio TX 78840

KD8AVS
David L Denman
109 Brinkley Cir
Del Rio TX 78840

KD5YAE
James L Sunderland Jr
115 Broadview
Del Rio TX 78840

KD5RRG
Mark B Essary
2511 Brodbent
Del Rio TX 78840

KD5RRH
Violet T Essary
2511 Brodbent
Del Rio TX 78840

KD5YAK
Janice D Manis
230 Burge Dr
Del Rio TX 78840

KC5LYB
Lana K Sutherland
120 Caballo Dr
Del Rio TX 78840

KE5MQG
Fernando Perez
149 Cerezo Ave Hcr2 Box 9
Del Rio TX 78840

KB5QIV
Jorge D Vargas
904 Clayton
Del Rio TX 78840

KB5PQI
Marilyn R Casson
111 Crosswinds
Del Rio TX 78840

KC5ZCQ
Leticia C Tamez
108 Danielle Dr
Del Rio TX 78840

KC5MOT

Aldo Calvetti
207 Dennis Dr
Del Rio TX 78840

KC5FNY
Robert I Palmer
1305 East 2nd St
Del Rio TX 78840

KD5SEW
Kevin L Van Hoozier
907 East 3rd
Del Rio TX 78840

KB5EJX
David J Flores
909 East 3rd St
Del Rio TX 78840

KC5FHS
Ricardo G Bermea
607 East 5th St
Del Rio TX 78840

KC5LNC
Diana Gonzalez
809 East 6th St
Del Rio TX 78840

KD5LHS
Angelo B Gonzalez
809 East 6th St
Del Rio TX 78840

N0CUV
Bruce A Crockett
606 East 8th Apt 407
Del Rio TX 78840

KD5YAJ
Daniel Reyes Jr
309 East Bowie
Del Rio TX 78840

KD5LHR
James E Babb
Hwy 90 East Box 1B
Del Rio TX 78840

KD5YAI
James Riddle
414 East Greenwood St
Del Rio TX 78840

KD5YAG
Ramiro Dominguez
213 East Rodriguez
Del Rio TX 78840

KB5QJV
Cesar G Rivera
207 East Viesca
Del Rio TX 78840

KB5QJX
Jesus Morales
405 Eduardo St
Del Rio TX 78840

N5UAA
Clouis H Hansen
216 Elizabeth Dr
Del Rio TX 78840

KD5TAR
Nicholas A Campiglia
209C Fletcher Dr
Del Rio TX 78840

W5BSO
William B Estes
313 Fox Dr
Del Rio TX 78840

N5PJR
Murry M Kachel
1010 Fury Creek Trl
Del Rio TX 788408506

KE5PWS
Jerry R Morrison
134 Garden Crest
Del Rio TX 78840

KF5GMM
Harmony D Mones-Murphy
144 Harvey Dr
Del Rio TX 78840

N5WRW
Dwight L Brown
317 Inspiration Way
Del Rio TX 78840

KA5MZK
Marion W Roberts
121 Jodobo Dr
Del Rio TX 78840

W5FTL
Albert J Klapetzky
7A June Ave
Del Rio TX 78840

KA5YIY
Maury G Thomas
468 Kelly Rd
Del Rio TX 78840

W5RWT
Maury G Thomas
468 Kelly Rd
Del Rio TX 78840

KB5PQU
Peter A Reyes Jr
115 Kim Dr
Del Rio TX 78840

KB5PTZ
Pedro A Reyes
115 Kim Dr
Del Rio TX 78840

KB5EJY
Mary S Young
104 King Henry Pl
Del Rio TX 78840

NF3F
Herschel E Rollins Jr
117 La Paloma Dr
Del Rio TX 78840

KE5QIU
Arthur F Flint
103 Lantana Ln
Del Rio TX 78840

KC7QGL
Ramon M Andrade
106 Lilac Ln
Del Rio TX 78840

KC5FLU
Raymond A Hazel
207 Margaret Ln
Del Rio TX 78840

KC5ZCZ
Ciro M Villarreal
308 Meandering

Del Rio TX 78840

KC5ZDA
Maria R Villarreal
308 Meandering
Del Rio TX 78840

KF6AHC
James H Murray II
104 Meandering Way
Del Rio TX 78840

KC5ZCP
Lisa V Villarreal
308 Meandering Way
Del Rio TX 78840

KB5INI
Raymond F Liehr
83 Miller Dr
Del Rio TX 78840

KD5YAP
Lavell S Barrera
103 North Frank St
Del Rio TX 78840

KB5QJT
Pedro D Salas
1311 North Main
Del Rio TX 78840

KB5QJY
Jesus Chavez
2406 North Main
Del Rio TX 78840

K5MBU
Mario Bosquez Sr
139 Northhill Dr
Del Rio TX 78840

N5VZJ
Jesus M Sandoval
135 Northill
Del Rio TX 78840

KE5OMB
John L Howley
125 Northill Dr
Del Rio TX 78840

K5KES
Wayne A Casson

115 Park Ave
Del Rio TX 788403932

N5YUP
Rodolfo C Benavidez
207 Peacepipe Tr
Del Rio TX 78840

KB5EDC
Roberto Fuentes Jr
1010 Pecan St
Del Rio TX 78840

KD5GMQ
James F Hoback
200 Quail Creek Dr
Del Rio TX 788402109

KF5AJB
Lee Jenkins
1000 Qualia Dr
Del Rio TX 78840

KB5YVX
Alejandro T Garcia Sr
117 Riata Dr
Del Rio TX 78840

WB5TZJ
Norman R Brines
113 Ridgemont
Del Rio TX 788403029

KD5YAM
Joann Cervantes
126 Ridgewood
Del Rio TX 78840

KB5LFQ
Layson K White
SR 1 Box 11 Rough Canyon
Area
Del Rio TX 78840

KD5HDH
James W Norvell
408 Rubio St
Del Rio TX 78840

KC0HUQ
Gregory M Moulton
211 Running Bear Trl
Del Rio TX 78840

KD5HQL
Marco A Nunez
546 Sage Hill Dr
Del Rio TX 78840

KE5FKT
Terry W Simons
1906 San Pedro
Del Rio TX 78840

KE5KQB
Daniel M Simons
1906 San Pedro Rd
Del Rio TX 78840

WD5EPC
Harold D Hoffman Jr
100 Smith Rd
Del Rio TX 78840

N5UFV
A D'Wayne Jernigan
107 South Broadview
Del Rio TX 78840

KB5PQP
Anson A Luna
107 South Broadview St
Del Rio TX 788402451

N9QOG
Dirk W Sykes
200 Space Blvd
Del Rio TX 788421717

KD5WBE
Jesus Sulaica Jr
307 Stricklen
Del Rio TX 78840

KA5PEC
Phyllis E Dugan
703 Stricklen Ave
Del Rio TX 78840

W5PWD
Phyllis E Dugan
703 Stricklen Ave
Del Rio TX 78840

KA5GKO
Patrick Dugan
703 Stricklen Ave
Del Rio TX 788402324

W5CPD
Patrick Dugan
703 Stricklen Ave
Del Rio TX 788402324

N0IIE
Grant C Bucks
240 Tomahawk Trl
Del Rio TX 78840

KE5RAH
Jose G Guerrero Martinez
807 B Veteras Blvd Pmb 120
Del Rio TX 78840

KB5QKQ
Cesar Calderon H
207 West 1st St
Del Rio TX 78840

KB5QJW
Josie L Morales
409 West 1st St
Del Rio TX 78840

KD5CUE
Kurt A Hill
201 West 2nd St
Del Rio TX 78840

W5JAA
James M Reagan
301 West 2nd St
Del Rio TX 78840

KD5YAF
Jose R Faz
808 West 3rd
Del Rio TX 78840

KD5YAN
Robert L Thornsburg II
304 West 4th
Del Rio TX 78840

KD5SEQ
Jesus C Lopez
409 West 6th St
Del Rio TX 78840

KB5QJZ
Timothy W Alarcon
202 West 7th St

Del Rio TX 78840

KD5SEP
Abraham J Lopez
307 West 9th
Del Rio TX 78840

KD5YAQ
Jesus Nava
305 West Gutierrez
Del Rio TX 78840

KB5QIT
Melisa Salas
902 West Gutierrez
Del Rio TX 78840

KD5YAO
Jesus Cardenas Jr
503 West Viesca
Del Rio TX 78840

KB5RZL
Daniel R Wisdom
Del Rio TX 78840

KD5SER
Robert D Norton
Del Rio TX 78840

NL7CD
Judith A Nicolas
Del Rio TX 78840

WA5DRW
Daniel R Wisdom
Del Rio TX 78840

KB5DRI
William D Petitt
Del Rio TX 78841

KB5PQS
Albesa I Jernigan
Del Rio TX 78841

KB5PQT
Monica L Calvetti
Del Rio TX 78841

KB5YUZ
Raymond W Miller
Del Rio TX 78841

KD5RRE
Keith D Brooks
Del Rio TX 78841

N5FHA
Sidney E Petitt
Del Rio TX 78841

N5YPJ
Richard D'Avy
Del Rio TX 78841

KD5SEL
Dora E Cerny
Del Rio TX 78842

KD5SEM
Katie K Clark
Del Rio TX 78842

KD5SES
Joe H Skelton
Del Rio TX 78842

KD5SET
Ralph N Skelton
Del Rio TX 78842

KD5SEU
James L Sunderland Sr
Del Rio TX 78842

KD5SEV
Jennifer L Sunderland
Del Rio TX 78842

KO5M
Shirley D Durham
Del Rio TX 78842

WP4NBP
Steven D Brimmer
Del Rio TX 78842

AH6AD
Paul L Nicolas
Del Rio TX 78844

KD5GHJ
Peter D Coggi
Del Rio TX 788410343

KJ5AQ
David R Wisdom

Del Rio TX 788411941

W5DRW
David R Wisdom
Del Rio TX 788411941

K5CXR
Joseph F Colvin
Del Rio TX 788420142

KD5SRE
Stephyn W Ramsey
Del Rio TX 788420622

KB5LJF
William J Beamesderfer
Del Rio TX 78840

WB6BCW
William D Van Nolan
Del Rio TX 78840

KB5PQG
Terry J Proctor
Del Rio TX 78841

FCC Amateur Radio Licenses in Dell City

KB5ZJW
Chancy E Harbolt
Dell City TX 79837

KD5EUA
Kathleen H Harbolt
Dell City TX 79837

FCC Amateur Radio Licenses in El Paso

AC5OE
Owen M Williamson
5817 Acacia Cir 714
El Paso TX 79912

AE5ZG
Jonas M Williamson
5817 Acacia Cir 714
El Paso TX 79912

KB5VEI
Jonas M Williamson
5817 Acacia Cir 714
El Paso TX 79912

KC5ZLQ
Gabriel Moreno
7504 Acapulco
El Paso TX 79915

KE5QKK
Osvaldo Ochoa
10000 Acer
El Paso TX 79925

KB5UDZ
Gil P Magayanes
9535 Acer 1001
El Paso TX 79925

KB5GAM
Ann Marie Szeredy
9905 Agena Ln
El Paso TX 79924

KF5NCP
Cody A Clark
613 Agua Caliente
El Paso TX 79912

KB5OMD
Jeremy D Miller
668 Agua Caliente
El Paso TX 79912

KD5ZBH
Reynaldo Luevano
740 Agua Caliente
El Paso TX 79912

KE7EQI
Jorge A Nava
641 Agua Del Rio
El Paso TX 79928

KM5RQ
Maynard Jackson
9849 B4 Alameda
El Paso TX 79927

KF5JJL
Peter Gingter
2417 Alan Ducan
El Paso TX 79936

W5NMR
Peter Gingter
2417 Alan Ducan

El Paso TX 79936

KE5AXW
Jann Antons
2417 Alan Duncan Ln
El Paso TX 79936

N5NMR
Jann Antons
2417 Alan Duncan Ln
El Paso TX 79936

KB5FTY
Ramon L Lake
9621 Album
El Paso TX 79925

N5EIN
Geraldine Hedrick
8044 Algerita
El Paso TX 79915

KB5QV
Jack E Hedrick
8044 Algerita
El Paso TX 799154638

KB5JAN
Roberto M Melendez Sr
5020 Alps Dr
El Paso TX 79904

N5WPR
Walter P Marschall
7116 Alto Rey
El Paso TX 79912

N5TAD
Neil Waxman
7120 Alto Rey
El Paso TX 79912

N5TAE
Pamela M Waxman
7120 Alto Rey
El Paso TX 79912

N5WPS
Andrew C Waxman
7120 Alto Rey
El Paso TX 79912

N5WPT
David R Waxman

7120 Alto Rey
El Paso TX 79912

N5MEM
Obaldo Garcia
3111 Altura Ave
El Paso TX 79930

KE5ZMZ
Oscar E Ontiveros
4329 Altura Ave
El Paso TX 79903

KD5JOT
Michael Tarnovsky
4613 Ambassador
El Paso TX 79924

N5OUM
Judith E Ferguson
6513 Amposta
El Paso TX 79912

KC5EEH
Jim K Mc Cain
1736 Andy Williams
El Paso TX 79936

KF5HUS
Allen L Yakubovsky
3513 Angle Face
El Paso TX 79936

KC5FIK
Norman L Bliss
9020 Ankerson
El Paso TX 79904

K0BIT
Peter W Dahl
5325 Annette Ave
El Paso TX 79924

W5LTS
Gerald R H Sanders
5106 Antonio
El Paso TX 79924

KB5NEQ
Alejandro Castillo
10745 Aquamarine
El Paso TX 79924

KC5IOK

Ima M Mc Aleer
6220 Arapaho
El Paso TX 79905

W5DEQ
John K Mc Aleer
6220 Arapaho Rd
El Paso TX 79905

KD5SWC
Jonathan Mendez
2516 Arizona
El Paso TX 79930

KC5EEE
Manuel Cobos
10813 Arlene Cir
El Paso TX 79927

KD5EKY
Beverly B Porter
10058 Arnold Dr
El Paso TX 799083087

WB5FZN
Dale N Richardson Sr
5621 Arrowhead Dr
El Paso TX 79924

N5EIT
Floyd M Coleman
3721 Atlas
El Paso TX 79904

KB5NCS
Victor J Reza
2728 Aurora
El Paso TX 79930

N5IZE
Raynold B Gillespie
3517 Aurora
El Paso TX 79930

KC2GVS
Rudolph T Ault
1401 Avalon Dr Apt B
El Paso TX 79925

K5UGR
Leland C Brookbank
681 Bailey Rd
El Paso TX 79932

KD5IKL
Rafael E Sanchez
7108 Banana Tree Ln
El Paso TX 79915

KE5OIA
Elizabeth A Crum
6078 Bandolero
El Paso TX 79912

AJ8E
Darwin R Crum II
6078 Bandolero Dr
El Paso TX 79912

KD5MUG
Darwin R Crum II
6078 Bandolero Dr
El Paso TX 79912

NK5V
James H Kluetz
5352 Bastille
El Paso TX 79924

W5MRW
Legette Stanton
5336 Bastille Ave
El Paso TX 79924

KB5NGV
Dionicio R Rivera
11400 Beach Front
El Paso TX 79936

KB5NGW
Irish Faye V Rivera
11400 Beach Front
El Paso TX 79936

KA5ZPS
Donna M Naylor
3316 Beachcomber Dr
El Paso TX 799361927

WA5RVE
Stephen E Naylor
3316 Beachcomber Dr
El Paso TX 799361927

N5PID
Croft Von Schuriach Obrada
5611 Beacon Ave
El Paso TX 79905

KE5ZMV
Christopher Whetten
6533 Bear Cat Ridge
El Paso TX 79912

KD5CGG
Gary S Anaya
5700 Beaumont Pl
El Paso TX 799125341

N5QJK
Paul B Agner
5725 Beaumont Pl
El Paso TX 79912

KB5KME
Roy B Sinclair Jr
600 Beechnut Rd
El Paso TX 79912

KE5FTN
Roy B Sinclair Jr
600 Beechnut Rd
El Paso TX 79912

KD5MEP
Lothar H Molarski Sr
10901 Bella Vista Dr
El Paso TX 79935

WA5KKY
Walter L Winfield
6024 Belladonna Cir
El Paso TX 79924

KC5IAD
Jay L Byler
218 Belvidere
El Paso TX 79912

AE5RJ
Reiner Junge
1216 Belvidere
El Paso TX 79912

KC5WDQ
Reiner Junge
1216 Belvidere
El Paso TX 79912

W6SYV
Russell W Parker
1417 Belvidere

El Paso TX 799121802

WA2BLH
Michael I Levine
1575 Belvidere St Apt 100
El Paso TX 79912

WA5MOT
Oscar Pilhoefer
1534 Bengal Dr
El Paso TX 79935

KC5KTM
Antonio E Ochoa Jr
11300 Benny Emler
El Paso TX 79934

KB5NJL
Helen E Goodson
816 Bergerac
El Paso TX 79907

N8IUW
George K Wright
10140 Bermuda
El Paso TX 79925

KB5RAH
Gilbert Hernandez Jr
10208 Bermuda
El Paso TX 79925

K5CEW
Carl E Womack
10213 Bermuda
El Paso TX 799255502

KD5MQL
Carl E Womack
10213 Bermuda
El Paso TX 799255502

KB5UDC
Robert Springer
10244 Bermuda Ave
El Paso TX 79925

N5EOV
Hester D Faulkenberry
218 Bernadine
El Paso TX 79915

K6QPZ
Patrick J Mc Auliffe

3120 Bert Yancey Dr
El Paso TX 79936

KI5DH
Orlando M Unruh
8000 Bethany Dr
El Paso TX 79925

N5XNE
Georgia S Unruh
8000 Bethany Dr
El Paso TX 79925

N5XIF
David Miramontes
7416 Big Bend Dr
El Paso TX 79904

KF5MHT
Michael C Larson
12301 Bill Mitchell Dr
El Paso TX 79938

K5HRS
Chris D Casner
1597 Billie Marie
El Paso TX 79936

KB5IWJ
Janice H Olson
1705 Bing Crosby
El Paso TX 79936

KB5EZV
James M Easter
325 Bird Ave
El Paso TX 79922

KA5KBG
Gary P Dubrosky
10316 Biscaine St
El Paso TX 799242904

K7ZGQ
John M Williams
3018B Bishop St
El Paso TX 79904

KE7ZGQ
John M Williams
3018B Bishop St
El Paso TX 79904

KB3HOF

Greta B Duran
3915 Bliss Ave
El Paso TX 79903

N3ZRR
Robert A Duran
3915 Bliss Ave
El Paso TX 79903

AB5TZ
Alvin L Hand
9628 Blue Wing Dr
El Paso TX 79924

WD5DQL
Steven J Alred
9808 Bluewing
El Paso TX 79924

KD5ZDI
 Veterans Amateur Radio Club
9628 Bluewing Dr
El Paso TX 79924

WA5VA
 Veterans Amateur Radio Club
9628 Bluewing Dr
El Paso TX 79924

KC0GQO
Chris C Houston Jr
9800 Bluewing Dr
El Paso TX 79924

KE5DHA
Sharon L Harris
9800 Bluewing Dr
El Paso TX 79924

KE5DHB
James E Harris
9800 Bluewing Dr
El Paso TX 79924

KE5ZMM
Alfred E White
749 Bluff Canyon
El Paso TX 79912

K5IHY
William T Bartlett
725 Bluff Canyon Cir
El Paso TX 79912

K9OAJ
Mark S Graham
2008 Bob Gilder Pl
El Paso TX 79936

KD5ICS
Larry D Grijalva
1500 Bob Hope Dr Apt 1201
El Paso TX 79936

K5ZL
Stanley D Shaw
11360 Bob Mitchell
El Paso TX 79936

KB5NEO
Antonio T Carrasco
5829 Bob White
El Paso TX 79924

KE5ZML
Steven T Soderborg Jr
5905 Bob White Ave
El Paso TX 79924

KE5ZPF
Carla R Smith
14798 Bombay Ct
El Paso TX 79928

KK5JX
Joseph C Oberndorfer
10236 Bon Aire
El Paso TX 79924

KA9NCO
Clifford R Andree
10175 Bon Aire Dr
El Paso TX 79924

KE5KJG
Clifford R Andree
10175 Bon Aire Dr
El Paso TX 79924

KF5GQG
Bobby L Akins
13150 Boots Greenrd
El Paso TX 79938

W5BLA
Bobby L Akins
13150 Boots Greenrd
El Paso TX 79938

W5KBP
James Trevo Mc Nutt
425 Borealis
El Paso TX 79912

KJ5EO
Herbert W Gehring III
 Box 12553
El Paso TX 79913

KE5HI
Thomas W Freeman
2717 Brady Pl
El Paso TX 79935

KC5GEH
George B Dye Jr
5024 Bragg Ave
El Paso TX 79904

W5NPI
Vasco C Rhoden Jr
5207 Brannon St
El Paso TX 79924

N5KII
Theodore E Wasko
9312 Breish Ct
El Paso TX 79925

N2ITO
Lawrence F Kenney
6604 Brisa Del Mar Dr
El Paso TX 79912

KF5JZS
Roland J Leon Sr
10523 Brisbane Way
El Paso TX 79924

KF5KMH
Roland J Leon Sr
10523 Brisbane Way
El Paso TX 79924

W5RJL
Roland J Leon Sr
10523 Brisbane Way
El Paso TX 79924

KC5BLC
Matthew F M Frank
4124 Broaddus Ave Rear

El Paso TX 799040577

K5JMW
John M Whitney
6552 Brook Ridge Cir
El Paso TX 79912

KE5ZEA
John M Whitney
6552 Brook Ridge Cir
El Paso TX 79912

KB5FSP
Garry J Collins
5181 Buffalo Creek
El Paso TX 79938

KC5NLQ
Guillermo Rodriguez
5161 Buffalo Creek Dr
El Paso TX 79938

W5RFU
Arvil B Collins
5181 Buffalo Creek Dr
El Paso TX 799388230

KB5HIF
Sara E Bernal
11429 Bunky Henry Ln
El Paso TX 79936

KB5KYA
Patrick R Rodriguez
6508 Byron
El Paso TX 79904

W5MXW
Walter S Walters
6408 Byron Ave
El Paso TX 79904

KA5MXC
Patricia U Mc Quien
10230 Byway
El Paso TX 79925

WB5IHE
Richard E Mc Kinnon Sr
10705 Bywood Dr
El Paso TX 79935

AD5PG
Charles G Bouton

10917 Bywood Dr
El Paso TX 79936

KE5YU
Hubert T Weatherford
4520 C J Levan Ct
El Paso TX 799246003

W5VYD
Jack R Rye
6024 Cadiz
El Paso TX 79912

N5PTA
Charles D Crepas
6105 Cadiz
El Paso TX 79912

KD5MEO
James R Loflin
6020 Camino Alegre
El Paso TX 799122606

KE5IHF
Chau D Watkins
6723 Camino Fuente
El Paso TX 79912

KC5TZS
Juan A Flones
10711 Candigan
El Paso TX 79935

KE5TX
William L Petroff
7921 Candlewood
El Paso TX 79925

AI0OK
Charles Gaunce
202 Canyon Terrace Dr
El Paso TX 79902

KA5UPM
Charles Gaunce
202 Canyon Terrace Dr
El Paso TX 79902

KE5ZMT
Blake D Larsen
317 Caporal Ct
El Paso TX 79932

KD5AQA

James T Lemaster
6232 Caprock
El Paso TX 79912

N5CFF
James T Clark
10612 Capt Valtr Dr
El Paso TX 79924

KB5IWG
Darrell F Becker
10312 Cardigan Dr
El Paso TX 79925

KB5HIB
Mario A Torres
244 Caribe
El Paso TX 79927

W2MMM
Mendle M Goldberg
5317 Carousel Dr
El Paso TX 79912

KC5ALD
Don R Carnline
5213 Carousel Dr 4
El Paso TX 79912

KJ4QES
David B Brown
13085 Carswell Ct
El Paso TX 79908

K5IE
Robert J Carroll Sr
10108 Castletown Dr
El Paso TX 799252912

N5LDZ
George L Sears
1564 Catham Cir
El Paso TX 79927

KA5TQF
David C Zulawski
2808 Catnip St
El Paso TX 799255212

KF5NZG
Willard L Sensiba
3013 Catnip St
El Paso TX 79925

KB5HPT
Lewis D Maxwell
10449 Centaur Dr
El Paso TX 79924

KE5YMG
Dean A Larson
4913 Century Way
El Paso TX 79924

WB5KFU
Randolph S Murray Jr
720 Cervantes Ct
El Paso TX 79922

KA5YGI
Rupert B Guard Jr
10544 Champlain
El Paso TX 79924

KC5BUJ
Garry W Moore Sr
3211B Chandler St
El Paso TX 79904

KG5PJ
Eugenio E Munguia
9401 Chantilly
El Paso TX 79907

KA5PAJ
William D Simpson
704 Chelsea St
El Paso TX 799035305

N5COI
Charles C Hardesty
344 Chermont Dr
El Paso TX 79912

KM5JT
Jesse J Smith
5825 Chippendale
El Paso TX 79934

N5FHO
Pat J Brown
7108 Cielo Vista Dr
El Paso TX 79925

K5AKR
John M Sharp
611 Cincinnati
El Paso TX 79902

K5UZT
J B Henderson
1102 Cincinnati
El Paso TX 79902

KB5NBR
Don L Wofford
5368 Circus Ln
El Paso TX 79912

KB5HPU
Alan J Jabale
305 Clairemont
El Paso TX 79912

WG6T
William G Durrer
240 Clairemont Dr
El Paso TX 79912

WA5FBM
Donald E Evans Jr
1225 Clausen Dr
El Paso TX 79925

K5ZWF
John Peroni
10548 Clearwater
El Paso TX 79924

K5YUA
Melvin F Rogers
3812 Clifton Ave
El Paso TX 79903

KB5KXO
Hugo E Page
4431 Clifton Ave
El Paso TX 79903

KA5TRQ
John R Herd
6177 Cloudy Sky Dr
El Paso TX 79932

KB1IEH
Sheila K Cowie
5672 Colin Powell
El Paso TX 79934

KD5HLM
Shawn W Cowie
5672 Colin Powell

El Paso TX 79934

KB5JGA
Rowena H Leitch
120 Colina Alta
El Paso TX 79912

KB5JVL
Mark W Leitch
120 Colina Alta
El Paso TX 79912

N5KBY
Joe H Archambault
8436 Comet St
El Paso TX 79904

WB7A
Richard M Denny
1865 Copa De Oro
El Paso TX 79936

KC5FIH
Leo R Young
2227 Copper Ave
El Paso TX 77930

KE5FYB
Phillip A Viscon
10128 Cork Dr
El Paso TX 79925

WB5PYF
Jeaneen A Larson
5219 Cornell
El Paso TX 799245333

K5UZB
Marcus E Larson
5219 Cornell Ave
El Paso TX 799245333

AA5EA
Wallace C Foster
5300 Cornell Ave
El Paso TX 799244716

WB5FKC
Christian W Brakhage
3212 Cornwall
El Paso TX 79925

KD5QPC
Glenn S Keller

5809 Coronado Ridge
El Paso TX 79912

KD5LAU
Bonita L Innes
5421 Corsicana Ave
El Paso TX 79924

N5FHF
Grant A Innes
5421 Corsicana Ave
El Paso TX 79924

KB5WGU
John E Le Flohic
5528 Corsicana Ave
El Paso TX 79924

KE5YMH
Sholley A Cox
805 Cortijo Dr
El Paso TX 79912

KE5YMI
Michael J Cox
805 Cortijo Dr
El Paso TX 79912

KC5HFE
Byrl H Burdick III
5305 Cory Dr
El Paso TX 79932

KA5WAF
Joe C Dillon
3302 Craigo Ave
El Paso TX 79904

WB4OGY
Richard H Hollenbeck
10440 Crete Dr
El Paso TX 799241720

N5FZD
William W Snowhill
10432 Cronus
El Paso TX 79924

KD5GWO
Daniel R Baca
263 Crown Point
El Paso TX 79912

KE5ZED

John S Golden Jr
115 Crown Point Dr
El Paso TX 79912

K6RMF
Loren D Ryno
232 Crown Point Dr
El Paso TX 79912

KD5GBO
James W Tate
10601-D Cuatro Vistas
El Paso TX 79935

WB5BLI
Daniel Cedillos
9183 Cuernavaca
El Paso TX 79907

WA4QGA
Raymond D Beard
20 Cumberland Cir
El Paso TX 79903

WA3AYS
John C Polonchak
4729 Cumberland Cir
El Paso TX 79903

WB3ATO
Irene A Polonchak
4729 Cumberland Cir
El Paso TX 799031923

KF5KTW
Ryan P Gutierrez
2001 Curt Byrum
El Paso TX 79936

KB5AMA
William J Thompson
765 Dahlia Court
El Paso TX 79922

KC5ASE
Adela G Guzman
5415 Dailey
El Paso TX 79905

W3HHZ
Al Robinson
6305 Dakota Ridge Dr
El Paso TX 79912

KC5SPO
Paul D Bowden
1983 Dana Bree St
El Paso TX 79936

KB5HQS
Frank K Liedtke
1666 Daniels Ln
El Paso TX 79936

KE5GUX
Eric Liedtke
1666 Daniels Ln
El Paso TX 79936

KF5IWT
Jace K Melton
1682 Daniels Ln
El Paso TX 79936

K2CED
Charles E Dockens
12033 David Forti Dr
El Paso TX 79936

KF5CBD
Charles E Dockens
12033 David Forti Dr
El Paso TX 79936

KH7TL
Jesse L Carrington
5709 David M Brown Ct
El Paso TX 79934

KB5EZU
David B Dusing
10 De Leon B7
El Paso TX 79912

KC5GVA
James D East
112 De Leon Dr
El Paso TX 79912

W5DJB
Edward L Cazzola
724 De Leon Dr
El Paso TX 79912

KB5HQE
Anthony A Mc Lean
10 De Leon Dr Apt I-1
El Paso TX 799124560

KB5HCF
Yvonne De La Garza
412 De Vargas
El Paso TX 79905

KD5IPX
Weldon W Mathews
1776 Dean Jones
El Paso TX 79936

N5YBO
Bryan A Cotton
11425 Dean Refram
El Paso TX 79936

K5OSC
Robert L Lewis
1118 Del Rio St
El Paso TX 79915

KB5HXE
Anthony A Mc Lean Jr
10 Deleon Dr Apt I1
El Paso TX 79912

N5AAM
Anthony A Mc Lean Jr
10 Deleon Dr Apt I1
El Paso TX 799124560

KD5EOY
Dale H Taylor
10101 Dellwood
El Paso TX 79924

KE5NCK
Ted B Wingo
10101 Dellwood Dr
El Paso TX 79924

N0KGC
Jeri L Holt
10101 Dellwood Dr
El Paso TX 799243236

N5ICP
John E Hall
14625 H Derringer
El Paso TX 799389530

KD5MEM
Joel Enriquez
661 Desert Ash Dr

El Paso TX 79928

KD5MEN
Anabel Enriquez
661 Desert Ash Dr
El Paso TX 79928

KE5ACA
Ethan D Foster
1212 Desert Javel Dr
El Paso TX 79912

KB5VBQ
Joseph B Ries
7223 Desert Jewel
El Paso TX 79912

KD5ZBG
Duane M Shaw
1220 Desert Jewel Dr
El Paso TX 79912

WA5FVE
Oliver R Smith
9512 Desert Ridge
El Paso TX 79925

WB5DWJ
Joe R Silva
9537 Desert Ridge
El Paso TX 79925

KD5RU
Benny G Steagall
9501 Desert Ridge Dr
El Paso TX 79925

W5DBC
David B Camp Sr
5534 Desert Willow Dr
El Paso TX 79938

W5PDC
Patricia D Camp
5534 Desert Willow Dr
El Paso TX 79938

WD5HTQ
David B Camp Sr
5534 Desert Willow Dr
El Paso TX 79938

WD5HTR
Patricia D Camp

5534 Desert Willow Dr
El Paso TX 79938

WA5EPM
Jesse R La Fleur
3008 Devils Tower Cir
El Paso TX 79904

KC5EED
Patrick M Ballard
5712 Devon
El Paso TX 79924

N5XOR
Rodger D Ballard
5712 Devon Ave
El Paso TX 79924

KF5HLC
 Western Technical College Arc
9451 Diana Dr
El Paso TX 79924

KF5JHI
Roberto Valencia Jr
2109 Diciembre
El Paso TX 79935

WB0RTG
Brenda K Rutledge
11216 Dick Lotz Ln
El Paso TX 79936

KB5WGW
Armida Paredes
11825 Dick Mayers
El Paso TX 79936

KC5EEF
Eral Jamison III
1613 Dick Ritter
El Paso TX 79936

KD5ZVU
Rodolfo A Gutierrez
486A Dini Rosi Dr
El Paso TX 79927

K5FWN
Eugene P Justice
3303 Donegal
El Paso TX 79925

KF5EAJ

Gene M Tucker Sr
3306 Donegal Rd
El Paso TX 79925

N5LCR
Richard M Jage Jr
3320 Drumond Rd
El Paso TX 79925

KA5QGA
Thea M Dick
3030 Dublin
El Paso TX 79925

KC5GZM
Marcia J Merrell
3203 Dublin
El Paso TX 79925

KC5LPP
Marilyn J Merrell
3203 Dublin
El Paso TX 79925

NO5NO
Monique J Merrell
3203 Dublin
El Paso TX 79925

WA5HBX
John W Merrell
3203 Dublin St
El Paso TX 799254312

KB5RAA
Francisco Casanova Jr
10955 Duke Snider Cir
El Paso TX 79934

KA5KOP
Barry W Allison
870 Dulce Tierra
El Paso TX 79912

KC5UA
Charles M Barber
3341 Dungarvan Dr
El Paso TX 79925

NK5T
Mack Wilson
900 Duskin Dr
El Paso TX 79907

W5BFN
Walter M Liggett
9104 Duval
El Paso TX 79924

KC5EEJ
Francisco J Ramirez
10126 Dyer St
El Paso TX 79924

W5XE
William R Colbert
10414 Dyer St 17
El Paso TX 799242740

KK5VF
John B Collins
3005 Eads Pl
El Paso TX 79935

KA5MOA
Harold E Andrus
2908-C Eads Pl
El Paso TX 79935

KD5FLT
Ignacio R Gonzalez
5609 Eagle Poit
El Paso TX 79912

KD5MQM
Guy L Marangoni
1061 Eagle Ridge Dr
El Paso TX 79912

WB4KBP
Dennis W Campbell
1109 Eagle Ridge Dr
El Paso TX 799127476

KI4CWY
Michael S Anderson
6537 Eagle Ridge Dr
El Paso TX 799127434

KC5DYF
Edward E Woolley
311 East Franklin 109
El Paso TX 79901

N5OQL
Jesus D Valenzuela
1137 East Nevada
El Paso TX 79902

WB5ZGG
Rodolfo E Paniagua
1120 East Nevada Ave
El Paso TX 79902

N5XOP
Vincent V Giordano
1145 East Rio Grande
El Paso TX 79902

KB5JAJ
Charles N Clay
1110 East River
El Paso TX 79902

KD5DVW
Russell D Hawk
9780 Eastridge Dr
El Paso TX 799256816

K5DTP
John F Cram
9788 Eastridge Dr
El Paso TX 79925

N6TOC
Joel T Rodriguez
11169 Ebb Tide Dr
El Paso TX 79936

KF5EIL
Manfred A Knoepfle
6833 Echo Cliffs Dr
El Paso TX 79912

KD5DHK
Raymond Licon
8315 Eclipse
El Paso TX 79904

KB5HPW
Sean P Mc Guirk
7413 Edgemere
El Paso TX 79925

N5XOO
Patricia S Launspach
7913 Edgemere
El Paso TX 79925

WA5KYV
Charles B Wood
8713 Edgemere

El Paso TX 79925

WB5LVF
Richard L Olson
10865 Edgemere Apt G5
El Paso TX 79935

KE5ZPH
Lloyd A Schook
7204 Edgemere Blvd
El Paso TX 79925

N5FAZ
Paul H Launspach
7913 Edgemere Blvd
El Paso TX 799253836

N0HDH
Bobby D Medley
8009 Edgemere Blvd
El Paso TX 79925

N5GYC
Paschal O Wesley Jr
5116 Edmonton Ave
El Paso TX 799243304

WA5NJA
Charlie C Shane
4721 El Campo
El Paso TX 79924

W9SRA
Thomas J Le Sage
609 El Gusto St
El Paso TX 79912

KB5IZT
Simeon J Burtner
5725 El Nido Ct
El Paso TX 79905

KF5GID
Ryan A Munden
6701 El Parque
El Paso TX 79912

KF5LHW
Leon G Bean
605 El Parque Dr
El Paso TX 79912

KD5NBT
Stefan Kutz

717 El Pinal Pl
El Paso TX 79912

W5RDS
Richard D Southern
5347 El Quelite
El Paso TX 79932

KD5YOX
William D Thomas Jr
4730 Emory Rd
El Paso TX 79922

W5WDT
William D Thomas Jr
4730 Emory Rd
El Paso TX 79922

K5SHO
Ralph E Shorts Sr
4312 Emory St
El Paso TX 79922

WB3CKF
Ralph E Shorts Sr
4312 Emory St
El Paso TX 79922

KB5QZZ
Peter H Ku
10953 Ernie Banks
El Paso TX 79934

N5MJF
Craig G Jensen
6605 Escondido
El Paso TX 79912

W1FXK
Carleton M Dane
6601B Escondido
El Paso TX 79912

N5WAW
Stephen N Taylor
6212 Escondido Dr
El Paso TX 79912

KK5NQ
Sandra S Muns
724 C Espada Dr
El Paso TX 79912

W5UKM

Herman R Muns
724C Espada Dr
El Paso TX 79912

KB5PYN
John H Herron Jr
1031 Esplanada Cir
El Paso TX 79932

N5XNP
William A Carrier
1067 Esplanada Cir
El Paso TX 79932

KD5QAC
Joe Gonzalez
11004 Essex Falls Ln
El Paso TX 79934

WB6TGF
Richard P Shane
3416 Evalyn Ave
El Paso TX 799044530

KB5HHZ
Mirna L Bracamontes
9300 Fair Fax
El Paso TX 79924

W6FMS
Willie D West
4600 Fairbanks
El Paso TX 79924

N5PIF
Kelly W Mock
5205 Fairbanks 44
El Paso TX 79924

KB5KXN
Georgette M Lovelady
5255 Fairbanks Apt D
El Paso TX 79924

KB5KXP
James T Lovelady
5255 Fairbanks Apt D
El Paso TX 79924

KB5HIE
Dulce G Bracamontes
9300 Fairfax
El Paso TX 79924

N5FDC
Tim C Edgerly
1309 Fairfield Dr
El Paso TX 79925

KI5TN
Wolfgang Rasquin
512 Fanner Rd
El Paso TX 79916

N5SXG
Daniel G Condoni
3119 Federal
El Paso TX 79930

N5EJA
John M Matthews
3142 Federal
El Paso TX 79930

KA5ACK
Henry J Duchouquette
2704 Federal Ave
El Paso TX 799303104

KB5ZHL
Suzanne G Hunter
6752 Fiesta
El Paso TX 79912

KB5RAI
Joe C Palmer
1513 Fir
El Paso TX 79925

K5VI
Andrew A Hair
2817 Fir
El Paso TX 79925

W5QWD
John S Cole
2916 Fir
El Paso TX 79925

W5UED
Charles J Ernst
5401 Fleetwood Rd
El Paso TX 79932

KE5FYC
Manuel A Munoz
11710 Flor Del Rio
El Paso TX 79927

KB5NEN
William M Thompson II
5904 Flounder Dr
El Paso TX 79924

KD5IKN
Jim Mcphetridge III
228 Flynn Dr
El Paso TX 79932

KB5BGK
Gloria M Leon
239 Flynn Dr
El Paso TX 79932

KC5FFV
Jon S Buchynsky
14001 Fort Apache Ln
El Paso TX 79938

N5TZJ
George Shanahan
3109 Fort Blvd
El Paso TX 79930

KC5PUY
Kevin T Stansbery
3126 Fort Blvd
El Paso TX 79930

KB5MLO
Kelly E Plymale
44 Fountain Apt 15
El Paso TX 79912

AE5QN
Christopher B Woodworth
433 Francisco
El Paso TX 79912

KB5PDH
Stephen W Young
3718 Frankfort St
El Paso TX 79930

KE5ZMO
Lincoln C Smith
6412 Franklin Ridge
El Paso TX 79912

N6URJ
David O Flynn
6357 Franklin Trl

El Paso TX 79912

KB5YT
Ronald S Love
11741 Fred Perry
El Paso TX 79936

KC5KNS
William W Love
11741 Fred Perry
El Paso TX 79936

KB5HBT
Lorena F Moore
216 Fremont
El Paso TX 79912

N5RK
John B Moore Jr
216 Fremont
El Paso TX 79912

N5IAF
John D Bulger
405 Frontera
El Paso TX 79922

W5JUD
Judson L Caruthers
3308 Gabel
El Paso TX 79904

KD5RPY
Webster D Powell
9633 Gairloch Dr
El Paso TX 79925

KC5WSE
Robin L Bourdeau
10608 Galatea Pl
El Paso TX 79924

WA5UOO
Irma E Waltz
8810 Galena Dr
El Paso TX 79904

WB5VRF
William E Waltz
8810 Galena Dr
El Paso TX 79904

K5WAE
Pollard Rodgers

801 Galloway Dr
El Paso TX 79902

KF5HUT
Rosa M Manriquez
10056 Galveston Dr
El Paso TX 79924

K5ULI
Heinz-Ulrich U Landeck
10056 Galveston Dr
El Paso TX 79924

KE5UJE
Fernando Cervantes
9804 Gardenia Ct
El Paso TX 79925

KB5NBS
Edward A Eberhardt
5008 Garland Ln
El Paso TX 79924

KC5ALB
Joseph Lucero Sr
5111 Garland Ln
El Paso TX 79924

KF5NHF
Gerald E Held
3012 Gastor Dr
El Paso TX 79935

KE5ULU
Charles F Pine
7670 Gateway Blvd East Apt 22
El Paso TX 79915

AD5GF
Michael Tarnovsky
10330 Gateway Blvd North Apt
17D
El Paso TX 79924

KB5RPX
Rafael S Guillen
6001 Gateway West 255
El Paso TX 79925

N5SGU
Betty J Barter
2705 Gene Littler
El Paso TX 79936

N5SGW
Richard N Barter
2705 Gene Littler
El Paso TX 79936

AC5AL
Andrew J Wall
1605 George Dieter Pmb 648
El Paso TX 79936

N5NPD
Saeid S Hadavi
1650 George Dieter 801
El Paso TX 79936

KE5NCL
Victoria M Edwards
605 Gibson Veck Rd - Space -
39
El Paso TX 79922

N5YPS
Ruben Cobos
9896 Gifford Dr
El Paso TX 79927

AA7TJ
George R Bruner
14277 Gil Reyes Dr
El Paso TX 79938

N5HGG
William T Hall Jr
310 Golf View Ln
El Paso TX 79927

N5TRV
Daryl P Cooley
10044 Gcliad
El Paso TX 79924

W5URT
Noel C Olmstead
7304 Gocd Samaritan Ct 216
El Paso TX 79912

AE5MF
Richard L Rosario
12105 Gcya Ct
El Paso TX 79936

KE5UJG
Richard L Rosario
12105 Gcya Ct

El Paso TX 79936

W5VYB
Owen A Lehr
7731 Gran Quivira
El Paso TX 799043523

N5DAH
L Steve Ditmore
7125 Gran Vida
El Paso TX 79912

WD5DIP
Kenneth A Gorski
517 Granada
El Paso TX 79912

KF5HXR
Jim L Cox
6608 Grand Ridge Dr
El Paso TX 79912

K2JOQ
Eric V Schollmann
1029 Granite Trl Ct
El Paso TX 79912

K5HZH
Leonard Ullom
5627 Green Castle Rd
El Paso TX 79932

KE5ZNB
Karl T Murphy
729 Green Cove Dr
El Paso TX 79932

KE5ZPD
Luis A Loya
2083 Greenlee Dr
El Paso TX 79936

KB5NRI
Ronautta R Griffith
3720 Greenwich
El Paso TX 79902

WB5NHP
Randy E Edwards
10333 Grouse 163
El Paso TX 79924

W7LIH
John E Weber

10333 Grouse 17
El Paso TX 79924

KF6IJV
Marco A Amaya
14725 Gruenther Rd
El Paso TX 799388257

KC5QDG
Robert L Davis
9801 Gschwind
El Paso TX 79924

AE5NU
Dwight A Lavender
5004 Guido Ln
El Paso TX 79903

KE5ZSA
Dwight A Lavender
5004 Guido Ln
El Paso TX 79903

KG5LS
Leonard J Hanson
5403 Gulfport
El Paso TX 79924

KC5LUV
Jared E Cochrane
2753 Gunnison
El Paso TX 79904

N5EIL
Marion R Heald
3341 Guthrie
El Paso TX 79935

KF5CZT
Manuel A Arellano
11632 Gypsum Hills
El Paso TX 79936

W5DTP
John J Dunsmore
5204 Hanawalt Dr
El Paso TX 79903

KB5FRN
Andrew T Ruiz
2105 Happer St
El Paso TX 79903

WA5RGR

Thelma M Triplett
4748 Harcourt Dr
El Paso TX 79924

KB5HUF
Robert E Rice
5319 Harlan Dr
El Paso TX 79924

KB5DNO
Paul E Ferris
3016 Harrison
El Paso TX 79930

KD5HD
Edward D Bird
4717 Harvest Ln
El Paso TX 799241016

N5JLZ
Rufus R Humphries
4608 Hellas Dr
El Paso TX 799241735

KC5IAG
William A Steffen
7801 Hemlock St
El Paso TX 79925

WA5QCP
Richard L Kennedy
5633 Hemmingway
El Paso TX 79924

KE5IAG
Juan E Palos
3141 Hickman St
El Paso TX 79936

KC5IDV
Coston L Whatley Sr
3237 High Point
El Paso TX 79904

KE5HH
James W Hendley
3225 High Point Dr
El Paso TX 79904

WD9BMS
Sefton Mitchell
333 Higley Cir
El Paso TX 79927

KD5IPY
Cornelius K Blesius
3901 Hillcrest
El Paso TX 79902

KD5YCQ
Jeffrey P Chase
10468 Hodges Cir
El Paso TX 79924

KC5UPH
James D Hodges
10324 Holly Hock
El Paso TX 79924

KE5ZMR
Katharina I Rasquin
2120 Home Show Ln
El Paso TX 79936

KE5ZMQ
Matthias W Rasquin
2120 Home Show Ln
El Paso TX 79936

KD5TSR
Stephen P Preston Mr
5502 Hondo Pass   Wallace
Hughston Lodge
El Paso TX 79924

KC5JOO
Francis W Laverpool
4119 Hookheath Dr
El Paso TX 799221219

KE5WHM
James S Rivera
4202 Hookheath Dr
El Paso TX 79922

N5EPT
James S Rivera
4202 Hookheath Dr
El Paso TX 79922

KC5LPU
Jose L Snchez
8621 Hopewell
El Paso TX 79925

K5LJF
William C Hilbert
8712 Hopewell

El Paso TX 79925

W5VZG
Gerald J Servatius
8604 Hopewell Dr
El Paso TX 79925

KB5NGX
Amy A Guerra
2004 Howze
El Paso TX 79903

KF5KYO
Edward J Held
1525 Howze St
El Paso TX 79903

KE4SIW
Yeadon Smith
3221 Hueco Ave
El Paso TX 79903

KB5SQD
David Flores Sr
3712 Hueco Ave Rear
El Paso TX 79903

AI0X
Robert W Black Wolf
5033 Hueco Tanks Rd
El Paso TX 79938

KK5KI
Robert W Black Wolf
5033 Hueco Tanks Rd
El Paso TX 79938

NA0AI
Robert W Black Wolf
5033 Hueco Tanks Rd
El Paso TX 79938

KA5MJU
Daniel P Darling
5518 Husky Ct
El Paso TX 79924

KC5SPN
Rodolfo Calderon
3900 Idalia Ave
El Paso TX 79930

KD5IBD
Aaron J Williams

9213 Igoe
El Paso TX 79924

KB5MLW
Sean R Griffin
10064 Imperial
El Paso TX 79924

KE5KVI
Jeffrey A Riggs
11736 Imperial Gem Ave
El Paso TX 79936

KB5HXD
Chris Christensen
351 Innsbruck Ave
El Paso TX 79927

AB5OY
Bryan L Slayton
124 Isabella
El Paso TX 79912

W6LVB
Richard E Lauer
6613 Isla Del Rey
El Paso TX 79912

AB5HX
Henry T Uhrig
6717 Isla Del Rey
El Paso TX 79912

KB5TZS
Irene C Uhrig
6717 Isla Del Rey
El Paso TX 79912

W5RJC
George L Boley
10648 Islerock Apt
El Paso TX 79935

KB5AQR
Charles R Berry
11329 Jack Cupit Ln
El Paso TX 79936

WA5GGU
Horst H Hagemann
8702 Jade Ln
El Paso TX 79904

WA5GIO

Randell L Drovdahl
8708 Jade Ln
El Paso TX 79904

KD5QXU
Luis G Navarro Jr
10037 Jamaica St
El Paso TX 79924

AA5SI
Harold W Johnson Jr
11618 James Grant
El Paso TX 79936

N5IMZ
Scott E Segall
10604 Janway
El Paso TX 79935

K5LUG
John E Martin
10740 Janway Dr
El Paso TX 79935

WD5CUM
Mary L Martin
10740 Janway Dr
El Paso TX 79935

KC5KNT
Bruce M Janos
10700 Jason Way
El Paso TX 79935

KB5IZQ
John M Stage
1508 Jerry Pate
El Paso TX 79935

KG5QM
Loyal A Nance
10605 Jetrock Dr
El Paso TX 79935

KC5OEL
Antonio Dorado
13920 Jeweled Desert
El Paso TX 79928

KE5QMF
Charles Cody Maly
13912 Jeweled Desert Dr
El Paso TX 79928

KT5CCM
Charles Cody Maly
13912 Jeweled Desert Dr
El Paso TX 79928

KC5RHK
Ronald R Kowalzick
5221 Joe Herrera
El Paso TX 79924

KB5PXY
Jose Renteria Jr
1288 John Phelan
El Paso TX 79936

KE5BQK
Linda R Krasowski
11637 John Weir Dr
El Paso TX 79936

KD5QHV
Bernard G Krasowski
11637 John Weir Dr
El Paso TX 799364064

NP3NT
Radames Sanchez Jr
12465 Jon Evans Dr
El Paso TX 79938

KB5MCE
Jose A Contreras
5401 Joyce Cr
El Paso TX 79904

KE5KVH
Shawn M Deraps
3831 Judy Marie Ln
El Paso TX 79938

N5RWZ
Floyd L Draper
1800 Julia May
El Paso TX 79935

KF5NSI
Rex J Haley
4804 Junction
El Paso TX 79924

KE5OIB
Thomas L Faulkenberry
1713 Karl Wyler
El Paso TX 79936

N5ATE
Dargelo Caballero
10447 Kendall St
El Paso TX 79924

K5WAC
 Usaisc Fort Bliss
309 Kent Ave
El Paso TX 799221222

KC0WKY
James H Olbrisch
309 Kent Ave
El Paso TX 799221222

KD9KC
Michael P Olbrisch
309 Kent Ave
El Paso TX 799221222

N5NHC
Monika Olbrisch
309 Kent Ave
El Paso TX 799221222

KC5KTN
Enrique Mancha
15151 Kentwood
El Paso TX 79927

KB5FBF
Joseph Labus
10044 Kenworthy St
El Paso TX 79924

KB5BGP
Donald J Roberts
10324 Kenworthy St
El Paso TX 79924

K5TJC
Fred W Lampert Jr
420 Kenyon Joyce Ln
El Paso TX 79902

KA5ZLR
Bob W James
10049 Keystone Dr
El Paso TX 79924

KD5SAN
Bob W James
10049 Keystone Dr

El Paso TX 79924

W5TQT
Mauldin Finch
3218 Killarney
El Paso TX 79925

KE5KVK
Justin Rogers
3417 Killeen
El Paso TX 79936

K5AK
Ramon R Narad
14816 Kingston Rd
El Paso TX 79927

AK9B
Raymond E Morales Sr
14876 Kingston Rd
El Paso TX 799277226

N9EUN
Keiko Morales
14876 Kingston Rd
El Paso TX 799277226

KE5ZMS
John R Passow
308 Kingswood Dr
El Paso TX 79932

KE5UPF
Porfirio B Ramirez
12300 Kit Carson
El Paso TX 79936

WA5RHR
Betty J Hogwood
4290 Knag St
El Paso TX 79938

KC5YVD
Toby J Matthieu
6709 La Cadena
El Paso TX 79912

KD5FWU
Armando Uribe
6536 La Cadena Dr
El Paso TX 79912

N5IPA

US International Police
Association Radio Club
6816 La Cadena Dr
El Paso TX 79912

K5CW
Roland Mata
6816 La Cadena Dr
El Paso TX 799122810

K5CWO
Roland Mata
6816 La Cadena Dr
El Paso TX 799122810

K5EVA
Gabriela Mata
6816 La Cadena Dr
El Paso TX 799122810

K6CWO
Roland Mata
6816 La Cadena Dr
El Paso TX 799122810

K6NOW
Gabriela Mata
6816 La Cadena Dr
El Paso TX 799122810

KD5QWT
Carlos L Olivo
6824 La Cadena Dr
El Paso TX 79912

N5LVW
Richard O Baish
5440 La Estancia
El Paso TX 79932

KE5YME
Brett E Sanderson
6344 La Posta Dr
El Paso TX 79912

KE5YMF
David E Sanderson
6344 La Posta Dr
El Paso TX 79912

KF5CMV
Sheri K Sanderson
6344 La Posta Dr
El Paso TX 79912

KB5RG
Hedy K Schauer
5209 La Taste
El Paso TX 79924

KD5EFF
Charles C Clark
5224 La Taste Ave
El Paso TX 79924

WM8K
Marshall H Dean
5228 La Taste Ave
El Paso TX 79924

N5ISH
Wesley A Wilson
5308 La Taste Ave
El Paso TX 799244635

KC5JDI
Edward T Walsh
1205 Lafayette Dr
El Paso TX 799071215

K5KBE
Robert S Ferrell
9125 Lait
El Paso TX 79925

K5PHF
David A Clark
9225 Lait Dr
El Paso TX 79925

KC5NVF
Diana L Smith
2420 Lake Michigan
El Paso TX 79936

WT0K
Volker Winterscheid
10189 Lakeview
El Paso TX 79924

N5NRP
Everette F Coppock
10189 Lakeview
El Paso TX 799242945

KE5ASL
Wolfgang Mahlke
10189 Lakeview

El Paso TX 79924

N5QVQ
Edward Solomon
836 Lakeway
El Paso TX 79932

KD5JZS
Robert A Christenson
605 Lakeway Dr
El Paso TX 799323118

K5TAW
Terry A Ward
829 Lakeway Dr
El Paso TX 79932

KB7NTP
Terry A Ward
829 Lakeway Dr
El Paso TX 79932

KD5NAK
Terry A Ward
829 Lakeway Dr
El Paso TX 79932

KB5QZU
Marc I Hunter
628 Lakeway Dr
El Paso TX 79932

KA5CEM
Daniel E Fenton
1728 Larry Hinson
El Paso TX 79936

KB5NDC
Manuel E Medina
3004 Larry Wood Pl
El Paso TX 79936

K0BPC
Steven A Krueger
3730 Las Casitas
El Paso TX 79938

KC5QDF
Christopher A Poole
3509 Leavell Ave
El Paso TX 79904

WA5FCV
Harold C Hageman

9044 Leo St
El Paso TX 79904

KB5PPI
Luis Renteria
10237 Letona
El Paso TX 79927

KB5MHS
Walter D Winfield
1516 Likins Dr
El Paso TX 79925

WR5O
Walter D Winfield
1516 Likins Dr
El Paso TX 79925

KB5NOL
William C Elliott
3301 Lincoln Ave 10
El Paso TX 79930

KB5VEJ
Heriberto J Macias
1404 Linkins Dr
El Paso TX 79925

WB5IPU
Billy Sanchez
207 Little John
El Paso TX 79924

KD5KCX
Victor J Reza
10016 Lockerbie
El Paso TX 79925

W5SQM
Warren B Thwaites II
9940 Lockerbie Ave
El Paso TX 79925

KE5CGI
Brian J Bowden
4301 Loma De Oro
El Paso TX 79934

AC5XZ
William W West
4321 Loma De Oro Dr
El Paso TX 79934

KB5HK

William W West
4321 Loma De Oro Dr
El Paso TX 79934

N5OV
William W West
4321 Loma De Oro Dr
El Paso TX 799343710

W5CSM
David L Null
4360 Loma De Oro Dr
El Paso TX 79934

KD5CMF
Linfield Cox Jr
4640 Loma De Plata
El Paso TX 799343565

KD5GHM
Steve R Troxel
4733 Loma De Plata
El Paso TX 79934

KC5UFB
Shane G Todd
4756 Loma De Plata
El Paso TX 79934

KC4BAV
David K Frazee
4500 Loma Del Rey
El Paso TX 79934

KE5EUN
David L Null
4735 Loma Del Rey Cir
El Paso TX 79934

KF5LHV
Alexander M Kassim
4324 Loma Hermosa Dr
El Paso TX 79934

WB8LBZ
Larry L Springsteen
4404 Loma Suave Ln
El Paso TX 79934

W6KWK
Kenneth W Kuhblank Jr
4217 Loma Taurina Dr
El Paso TX 79934

KB5NGY
Joanna K Herr
1501 Lomaland 213
El Paso TX 79935

N5QJS
Thomas J Mc Kegver
1642 Lomaland 224
El Paso TX 79935

KE5TFY
Aaron L Jones
6216 London Bridge
El Paso TX 79934

KB5UDB
Don C Richardson
608 Londonderry Rd
El Paso TX 79907

KD5YZE
Bruce A Cozad
5601 Longview Cir
El Paso TX 79924

W5PIE
Richard L Rumbaugh
5660 Longview Cir
El Paso TX 79924

W5RO
Quarter Century Wireless Assn
Chapter 64
5660 Longview Cir
El Paso TX 79924

WA5PIE
Richard L Rumbaugh
5660 Longview Cir
El Paso TX 79924

WB5RLT
David Thompson
5668 Longview Cr
El Paso TX 79924

KB5JAK
Casey Z Thomas
3222 Lorne
El Paso TX 79925

KC5JGU
James S Anderson
6240 Los Altos

El Paso TX 79912

N5IOY
Robert M Scholz
6317 Los Bancos
El Paso TX 79912

WD5AAV
Richard T Miller
6077 Los Pueblos
El Paso TX 79968

WA5ELG
Mel I Levenson
6361 Los Robles St
El Paso TX 79912

AG4YV
Raymond C Rumpf Jr
6004 Los Siglos Dr
El Paso TX 79912

KB5JAY
Ronald L Hash
1641 Lou Graham
El Paso TX 79936

KD5FLV
Ray E Scalf
3401 Louisville Ave
El Paso TX 79930

KA5EZS
Janet A Holstein
4721 Lucy Dr
El Paso TX 79924

WD5CUG
Charles E Holstein
4721 Lucy Dr
El Paso TX 79924

N5OGK
Marilyn M Shook
10309 Luella Ave
El Paso TX 799254366

WD5FVQ
Charles R Shook
10309 Luella Ave
El Paso TX 799254366

N5BVU
Greg Littlefield

7129 Luz De Espejo Dr
El Paso TX 79912

KE5WML
Debra L Ward
7564 Luz De Lumbre
El Paso TX 79912

W5QEZ
William D Bowen
8343 Lynn Haven Ave
El Paso TX 79907

KC5CEV
Deborah K Craig
6248 Mamba
El Paso TX 79924

N5PQZ
Henry T Craig III
6248 Mamba Ct
El Paso TX 79924

KA5MVF
Jan K Wilkins
6021 Manila Dr
El Paso TX 79924

KB5NEM
Scott E Wilkins
6021 Manila Dr
El Paso TX 79924

NM5T
Thomas L Wilkins
6021 Manila Dr
El Paso TX 79924

KA5PYZ
Terry L Corbett
3280 Manny Aguilera Dr
El Paso TX 79936

KE5ZNA
Wade R Richardson
1417 Maple Ridge Way
El Paso TX 79912

N5GHN
Deborah L Reynolds
6833 Marble Canyon
El Paso TX 79912

NJ5W

Rick L Reynolds
6833 Marble Canyon
El Paso TX 79912

W5KWH
Charles W Palmer
8701 Marble Dr
El Paso TX 79904

K5MTA
Edna L Edwards
5108 Marcillus
El Paso TX 79924

W5JTY
Franklin E Edwards
5108 Marcillus St
El Paso TX 79924

KF5WR
Paul Liston
5224 Marie Tobin
El Paso TX 79924

KE5RAU
Anthony A Stuckwisch
5708 Marie Tobin
El Paso TX 79924

WB5LJO
Martin W Raue
5109 Marie Tobin Dr
El Paso TX 79924

K5KKO
William H Raue
5109 Marie Tobin Dr
El Paso TX 799247109

K5MZT
Junia L Polk
5720 Marie Tobin Dr
El Paso TX 79924

KA9QGS
Henry E Butler III
801 Marimba
El Paso TX 79912

KE5ZPG
Shauna L La Grange
3580 Mark Jason Dr
El Paso TX 79938

KC5YVC
Maria Y Riuas
758 Martha Gale
El Paso TX 79912

ND5RR
Ruben R Rivas
758 Martha Gale
El Paso TX 79912

KB5RTS
Beverly G Schwarzkopf
3204 Matagorda
El Paso TX 79936

N5LNC
Jean P Schwarzkopf
3204 Matagorda
El Paso TX 79936

KB5WGS
Jeffery E Greene
4807 Maureen Cir
El Paso TX 79924

KF5LUM
Brandon Olson
4861 Maureen Cir
El Paso TX 79924

KB6JYF
Michael W Olson
4861 Maureen Cr
El Paso TX 79924

K6SXA
James R Herndon
9108 Mayflower Ave
El Paso TX 79925

KB5LJN
Robert J Escalante
7516 Mazatlan
El Paso TX 79915

KD5CFC
Richard A Mitchell
7549 Mazatlan Dr
El Paso TX 79915

KE5CHA
Bobby D Medley
9265 McCabe
El Paso TX 79925

N0HDH
Bobby D Medley
9265 McCabe
El Paso TX 79925

WA5YZU
Glen L Hummels
9125 McCabe Dr
El Paso TX 79925

K3INI
Robert A Sherwood
9253 McCabe Dr
El Paso TX 79925

W5VOL
Robert A Sherwood
9253 McCabe Dr
El Paso TX 79925

KB5IXQ
Andrew C Medley
9265 McCabe Dr
El Paso TX 79925

KB5KZK
Milagros E Medley
9265 McCabe Dr
El Paso TX 79925

KC5RGN
Shannon T Kirkpatrick
3437 McClean
El Paso TX 79936

KG4TRI
James E Newman
8612 McFall Dr
El Paso TX 79925

N5NRQ
David E Hug
4916 McGregor
El Paso TX 79904

KD5BRS
Nanci L Maddux
719 McKelligon Dr
El Paso TX 79902

KD5RPZ
Danilo Haase
2425 Mckinley 46

El Paso TX 79930

KC5RHJ
Carl E Kirkpatrick
3437 Mclean
El Paso TX 79936

W2IBZ
Louis B Geis Jr
1601 McRae Blvd J6
El Paso TX 79925

N5KJP
Neil C Keith
1525 Meadowview Dr
El Paso TX 79925

KD5BCF
Enrique S Garza Sr
10717 Melinda
El Paso TX 79927

W5ESG
Enrique S Garza Sr
10717 Melinda
El Paso TX 79927

KA5UFO
Enrique Garza Jr
10717 Melinda St
El Paso TX 79927

N5XTO
Enrique Garza Jr
10717 Melinda St
El Paso TX 79927

K5AHS
Austin High School Amateur
Radio Club
3500 Memphis
El Paso TX 79930

KE5DRB
Austin High School Amateur
Radio Club
3500 Memphis
El Paso TX 79930

KE5ZPC
Daniel R Sherman
2629 Memphis Ave
El Paso TX 79930

KA5LXO
Bruce E Manvell
10009 Mercedes
El Paso TX 79924

WB7NPF
John P Conlon
10033 Mercedes St
El Paso TX 79924

KC5NLR
Daniel M Marsh
6708 Mesa Grande
El Paso TX 79912

KA5WAE
Frank J Wasson Jr
3216 Mesa Verde Ln
El Paso TX 799043013

K5BPQ
Samuel M Preckett
1308 Mescalero
El Paso TX 79925

AC5KE
Remedios P Loza
5432 Mickey Mantle Ave
El Paso TX 799343266

N5NZE
David R Cardenas
1816 Mike Hill Dr
El Paso TX 79936

KC5YPG
Nicole M James
10125 Milan St
El Paso TX 799144563

KB5WHL
William F Lewis
8009 Mineola
El Paso TX 79925

KB5BOG
Billijo S Porter
5704 Mira Grande
El Paso TX 79912

N5DWC
Leslie N Ruddock
5853 Mira Serena
El Paso TX 79912

N5ZN
Anibal Perez
13561 Miracerros Dr
El Paso TX 79849

KC5GZO
Mauricio Rodriguez
1430 Miracle Way Apt 10
El Paso TX 79925

KB5GMX
Enio G Jelihovschi
402A Mississippi St
El Paso TX 79902

KC5IOI
John H Colbey
9269 Mo Fall
El Paso TX 79925

N5XOC
Juan A Puentes
576 Mogollon Cir
El Paso TX 79912

N5BKH
Charles R Garber
7705 Mojave Dr
El Paso TX 799151518

KC5LAF
Preston L Gladd
4565 Monahans Dr
El Paso TX 79924

KB5AJG
Sharon E Gonzalez
6369 Monarch Dr
El Paso TX 79912

W2BFI
Manuel R Gonzalez
6369 Monarch Dr
El Paso TX 79912

KB5DCQ
Wilmer G Medlock
3312 Monroe Ave
El Paso TX 79930

WB8YXR
John L Selesky
12705 Montana Lot 318

El Paso TX 79938

WB5VMG
Troy C Bunn
14521 Montana 55
El Paso TX 79938

KD5OSK
Ralph Dominguez Jr
13976 Montana Ave
El Paso TX 79938

AL7Q
John E Hennessy Sr
701 Montana Ave 210
El Paso TX 799025305

KC5DKM
Loren L Pinamonte
12705 Montana Ave Sp 402
El Paso TX 79936

N5JOC
Mary K Murrah
11540 Montana Ave Trlr A32
El Paso TX 799361418

KD5LPQ
Gary E Wade
9235 Montgomery Dr
El Paso TX 79924

W5TEE
Edward S Fryzel Sr
9301 Montgomery Rd
El Paso TX 79924

KB5OLX
Xaxier Cordova
9509 Montwood Dr
El Paso TX 79925

KA5HAE
Claude E Barron
3314 Moonlight
El Paso TX 79904

KB5WHQ
Lee E Baumgardner
6022 Morning Glory
El Paso TX 79924

KB5IZR
Dorothy G Pettit

6412 Morningside
El Paso TX 79904

KB5WAP
Melvin R Sams
6441 Morningside
El Paso TX 79904

KB5DJJ
Max E Pettit
6412 Morningside Cir
El Paso TX 79904

K0ZRC
Ralph D Carlson
6729 Morningside Cir
El Paso TX 79904

KB5NOS
David S Grossmann
6412 Morningside Dr
El Paso TX 79904

WB5WIG
Lee C Thomas
1728 Mosswood
El Paso TX 79935

WB5WIH
James D Thomas
1728 Mosswood
El Paso TX 79935

KA5AST
Randall W Miller
8800 Mount Delano Dr
El Paso TX 799042232

WB5HIW
Jeffrey R Strom
9012 Mount San Berdu
El Paso TX 79904

WB5HIX
Raymond C Strom
9012 Mount San Berdu
El Paso TX 79904

WB5PEQ
Sharon P Strom
9012 Mount San Berdu
El Paso TX 79904

W5OVH

Amelia E Wise
8516 Mount Scott
El Paso TX 79904

KB5NBU
John D Nealis
3221 Mountain Ave
El Paso TX 79930

KB5GZZ
Albert A Ortiz
3429 Mountain Ave
El Paso TX 79930

W5BGK
E Hubert Ruble
3200 Mountain Ridge Dr
El Paso TX 799043907

N5UYZ
Robert N Welch
5213 Mumm Ln
El Paso TX 79924

KB5PXX
Rachel J Welch
5213 Mumm Ln
El Paso TX 799245319

KB5QAF
Diana E Welch
5213 Mumm Ln
El Paso TX 799245319

KS5B
Donald L Jones
5217 Mumm Ln
El Paso TX 79924

WD8EFB
Frank E Rourke
1831 Murchison Dr
El Paso TX 79902

WD8EFC
Reba A Rourke
1831 Murchison Dr
El Paso TX 79902

KB5IYF
Kemmie C Miller III
10516 Murphy St
El Paso TX 79924

KE5HFR
Raymundo Resendez III
7765 Mustang
El Paso TX 79915

KA5EPI
Armand Chavez
2411 Nations
El Paso TX 79930

KB5RMD
Alan C Branch
2904 Nations
El Paso TX 79930

KC5UHR
Kyle D Rudnick
4100 Nations Apt 3
El Paso TX 79930

AE5GP
Thomas Handforth
11113 Nautical Dr
El Paso TX 79936

KE5HAL
Thomas Handforth
11113 Nautical Dr
El Paso TX 79936

K5HRI
Robert D Rogers
6305 Navajo
El Paso TX 79925

KE5AHW
Clyde L Gay
8712 Neptune St
El Paso TX 79904

KC5WAN
Magdaleno Armenta Jr
11533 Nettie Rose Cr
El Paso TX 79936

KF5KUK
Teo D Hull
116 New Orleans Dr
El Paso TX 79912

N5HRD
Charles W Hiett
10365 Newport Dr
El Paso TX 79924

KA5ZLX
Nadine R Hiett
10365 Newport Dr
El Paso TX 799242612

KB5NBW
Billy R Briceno
1201 Night Hawk Dr
El Paso TX 79912

KD5GQR
Nicholas J Prince
7205 Nighthawk Dr
El Paso TX 79912

N5HDA
Wilma F Nail
230 Nogal Pl
El Paso TX 79915

K5GSA
George R Nail
230 Nogal Rd
El Paso TX 79907

AA5QE
Carlton D Pool
11636 Norman Montion
El Paso TX 79936

KB5LAH
John M West
2308 North Florence St
El Paso TX 79902

KC5BZF
Steven C Willson
2404 North Kansas
El Paso TX 79902

AC5AK
James A Shaheen
2509 North Kansas
El Paso TX 79902

KD5FMW
Amy B Chahine
2509 North Kansas
El Paso TX 79902

KI5UV
Michael A Aguilar
11405 North Loop

El Paso TX 79927

W5JQI
Algie A Felder
8564 North Loop Rd
El Paso TX 79907

KC6ZPF
Michael L Drennon
4645 North Mesa
El Paso TX 79912

KD5KFX
Helen M Arditti
4740 North Mesa 148
El Paso TX 79912

AA5XW
Peter V Franusic
7101 North Mesa 172
El Paso TX 79912

KE5IJM
Roxanna C Schwarzkopf
2626 North Mesa -319
El Paso TX 79902

KA5YIM
James M Harris
2626 North Mesa 328
El Paso TX 79902

KC5GTE
Robin L Levy
1617 North Mesa St
El Paso TX 79902

KC5GEK
Robert A Levy
1617D North Mesa St
El Paso TX 79902

KC5GKX
Phyllis B Levy
1617D North Mesa St
El Paso TX 79902

AD5WX
David C Ponevac
2628 North Mesa St -163
El Paso TX 79902

W5OP
Jean P Schwarzkopf

3800 North Mesa St A2
El Paso TX 79902

KF5JUF
Stephen W Borron
3800 North Mesa St Ste A2-507
El Paso TX 79902

W1SWB
Stephen W Borron
3800 North Mesa St Ste A2-507
El Paso TX 79902

KZ5PDQ
Roxanna C Schwarzkopf
3800 North Mesa St Suite A2
El Paso TX 79902

KC5IOJ
Ricky L Gatlin
1717 North Pieadras
El Paso TX 79930

KC5PFV
Insights Science Museum
505 North Santa Fe
El Paso TX 79901

K5YQL
Louis Casavantes
914 North Stanton
El Paso TX 79902

KF5GQH
Derrick A Garcia
2506 North Stanton
El Paso TX 79902

N5SUI
Agustin H Torres
4020 North Stanton
El Paso TX 79902

KB5MTY
Ori Brafman
4433 North Stanton T28
El Paso TX 79902

KD5XN
William J Kennedy
2843 North Yarbrough 11
El Paso TX 79925

WB5VMD

Jeffrey A Parker Mr
2829 North Yarbrough Apt 2
El Paso TX 79925

KB5VEH
June H Geis
3037 North Yarbrough Dr Apt 2
El Paso TX 79925

W5IBZ
Louis B Geis Jr
3037 North Yarbrough Dr Apt 2
El Paso TX 79925

N2QXP
Marc Ellman
1324 North Yarrough Dr
El Paso TX 79925

KC5ZLR
Francisco X Terrazas
3780 North Zaragosa Rd
El Paso TX 79938

AB5VJ
Daniel W Asbridge
237 Northbrook Court
El Paso TX 79932

K5VQN
Greer W Craig
312 Northwind
El Paso TX 79912

KE5BHT
Heidi N Wilden
8944 Norton 3
El Paso TX 79904

KE5JOP
Keith L Wilden
8944 Norton Apt 3
El Paso TX 79904

K5HMJ
Heriberto J Macias
1500 Nueces Way
El Paso TX 79925

KA2WRV
Robert R Schwarzkopf
1500 Nueces Way
El Paso TX 79925

KC6EDU
Herbert W Buckley Jr
12188 O Brady Pl
El Paso TX 79934

KE5CGZ
Andrea C Westover
4694 O Shea 7
El Paso TX 79938

KB5BDY
Laurance N Nickey
5725 Oak Cliff Dr
El Paso TX 79912

N6ZYN
Arturo Ye Jr
2100 Octubre Dr
El Paso TX 79935

KF5JCH
Manuel A Quinones
6052 Ojo De Agua
El Paso TX 79912

K5GFU
Edgar E Elliott
5409 Olson
El Paso TX 79903

K5UYB
Gene L Graham
10422 Omega Cir
El Paso TX 79924

WD5CUJ
Godfrey A Young
1501 Opossum Cir
El Paso TX 79927

KA5SUF
Lloyd A Saylor
5701 Orlando
El Paso TX 79924

KB5OOH
Opal C Harris
5706 Orlando Ln
El Paso TX 79924

KB5OMW
Jay Applegate
8921 Ortega
El Paso TX 79907

KB5IPH
David E Peterson
6337 Osage
El Paso TX 79925

W5DJM
Thomas J Bergen
248 Osaple
El Paso TX 79932

N4YFH
Steven H Pate
5877 Oscar Perez Ave
El Paso TX 79932

KD5IKM
Dolores A Melero
11017 Paducah Ave
El Paso TX 79936

N5PIH
Alejandro Melero
11017 Paducah Ave
El Paso TX 79936

KE5VV
Joseph F Moon
3221 Pagosa Ct
El Paso TX 79904

AD5QF
Robert H Marsh
10569 Palomino St
El Paso TX 79924

N5ERH
Robert H Marsh
10569 Palomino St
El Paso TX 79924

N5ERI
Linda D Marsh
10569 Palomino St
El Paso TX 79924

NB5O
Robert H Marsh
10569 Palomino St
El Paso TX 79924

NB5P
Linda D Marsh
10569 Palomino St

El Paso TX 79924

KB5BFC
Earl T Hughes III
5128 Paris Ave
El Paso TX 79924

W5TEJ
Earl T Hughes
5128 Paris Ave
El Paso TX 79924

WP4NQL
Jorge Guzman-Torres
1009 Park Dr
El Paso TX 799022442

KA0LOE
Valente Medina Jr
8517 Parkland
El Paso TX 79925

K5FZH
Joe S Barnes
9012 Parkland
El Paso TX 799254015

KB5RRA
Gilbert L Ruiz
7928 Parral Dr
El Paso TX 79915

KE5ZPE
Oscar Hernandez
1844 Paseo Real Cir
El Paso TX 79936

KC5VHO
Rainer W Alpert
11928 Paseo Real Cir
El Paso TX 79936

KD5MFS
Edward S Wood
6732 Paseo Redondo
El Paso TX 79912

KC5UIY
Martin Cornish
213 Paso Noble
El Paso TX 79912

KC5UIZ
Nellie M Cornish

213 Paso Noble
El Paso TX 79912

K5TRW
Cleyborn E Emert
109 Pasodale Rd
El Paso TX 79907

KA5EWJ
Mary E Emert
109 Pasodale Rd
El Paso TX 79907

WB5TRW
Mary E Emert
109 Pasodale Rd
El Paso TX 79907

KC5MKB
Jorgen Skovdal
705 Patio Feliz Ln
El Paso TX 79912

KI6LYC
James E Carson
10691 Pearl Sands Dr
El Paso TX 79924

KF5EIM
Marius Lipka
3541 Peerless Pl Apt 11 C
El Paso TX 79925

KF5EOD
West Texas Digital Radio Club
1829 Peidra Roja
El Paso TX 79936

W5ELP
West Texas Digital Radio Club
1829 Peidra Roja
El Paso TX 79936

KA5RLA
Carla R Smith
11985-G Pellicano 133
El Paso TX 79936

KB5WGV
Joe Melendez
374 Pendale Rd
El Paso TX 79907

KD5EYE

Robert J Garcia
1597 Pete Faulkner
El Paso TX 79936

KF5HGA
William R Barber
13900 Pete Larue
El Paso TX 79928

WS9A
Michael R Smith
633 Pete Payan Dr
El Paso TX 79912

KE5IJG
David A Knowles
19315 Phillip Bazaar
El Paso TX 79938

AE5HE
Doug M Garcia
1829 Piedra Roja
El Paso TX 79936

KE5NCM
Doug M Garcia
1829 Piedra Roja
El Paso TX 79936

KB5KXW
Wayne R Slaughter
2814 Pierce Ave
El Paso TX 79930

N5KXW
Calvin L Dees
5324 Pikes Peak Dr
El Paso TX 79904

KB5RTR
William R Cooper
524 Pinar Del Rio Dr
El Paso TX 799321912

KC5GEF
Terry W Funk
11136 Pink Coral Dr
El Paso TX 79936

WB6NAY
Stewart R Powell Sr
6121 Pino Real Dr
El Paso TX 79912

KB5QAG
Arthur Graves
10603 Pisces
El Paso TX 79924

KB5IUL
Jeffery A Evans
9568 Pistachio
El Paso TX 79924

KE5ZMH
Gerardo V Flores
2431 Pittsburgh Ave
El Paso TX 79930

KF5LRC
Cora L Medina
656 Platino Pl
El Paso TX 79928

KD6CUB
Sean E Gardner
1448 Plaza Verde
El Paso TX 79912

KF5EAK
Gabriella C Gardner
1448 Plaza Verde
El Paso TX 79912

KE5KVJ
Leslie D Smith
10744 Pleasant Hill Dr
El Paso TX 79924

W5VMX
John G Mc Ternan
9576 Poinciana
El Paso TX 79924

N5GHQ
Alfred P De Roulet
5612 Pollard St
El Paso TX 79904

K6NOE
Noe Nevarez
5620 Pollard St
El Paso TX 79904

KF5QJ
Alvie D Kellner
6031 Pompeii
El Paso TX 79924

KB5BGO
Richard A Merrill
10401 Ponderosa
El Paso TX 79924

KB5KWW
Albert A Gemoets Jr
3215 Porter
El Paso TX 79930

KD5JLO
Luis A Hernandez
11721 Prado Del Sol
El Paso TX 79936

KG5D
Alfred J Bray
1124 Prescott Dr
El Paso TX 79915

KA5WBJ
Howard E Rogers
5008 Prince Edward
El Paso TX 79924

K5FOB
David L Adams
5121 Prince Edward
El Paso TX 79924

KD5SGV
Timothy A Gamwell
5608 Prince Edward
El Paso TX 79924

KB5WGR
Elizabeth A Casarez
5636 Prince Edward
El Paso TX 79924

KD5CMG
Claire R Rogers
5008 Prince Edward Ave
El Paso TX 799243201

K5LA
Floyd I Chowning
5637 Prince Edward Ave
El Paso TX 79924

KB2OYE
Elke Cumming
712 Prospect St Apt 12

El Paso TX 77902

W7ANA
John M Rooney
3400 Proud Eagle Dr
El Paso TX 799361233

KC5GUZ
Rafael F Siqueiros
1134 Puerto Rico St
El Paso TX 79915

N5GLR
Dorotha Y Mc Adams
6145 Quail 904
El Paso TX 79924

KC0GVH
Walter E Brown III
6145 Quail Ave Sp137
El Paso TX 79924

KF5JUG
James W Heath
10800 Quartz St
El Paso TX 79924

KA5SAM
Bernard O Garcia Sr
10053 Quebec St
El Paso TX 79924

KF5KPA
Juan C Ortiz
3148 Queens Garden Cir
El Paso TX 79936

KB5QZX
Carlo H De Shouten Jr
4517 R J Lunn
El Paso TX 79924

KB5RAX
Aida M De Shouten
4517 R J Lunn
El Paso TX 79924

KC5LBW
Raines C Hayes Jr
4632 R L Shoemaker Dr
El Paso TX 79924

KF5LPK
Gabriel Garcia

10168 Racoon Dr
El Paso TX 79924

AA5OG
Dick F Still
9226 Raleigh
El Paso TX 79924

AA5Q
James R Bradshaw Jr
9308 Raleigh
El Paso TX 79924

KB5GTO
Anita A Price
9109 Raleigh Dr
El Paso TX 79924

WA5IVX
Ronald G Price
9109 Raleigh Dr
El Paso TX 799247231

KB5YMQ
Elsa G Price
9111 Raleigh Dr
El Paso TX 79924

K5KEB
Katherine E Bradshaw
9308 Raleigh Dr
El Paso TX 799247236

KC5DQG
Billy Cason
2009 Ralph Janes Pl
El Paso TX 79936

KC5WSG
James J Keller
7216 Ramada Dr
El Paso TX 79912

WB5JZI
Billy J Browder
9016 Rancich
El Paso TX 79904

KB5UEA
Peter C Saxman
900 Raynolds
El Paso TX 79903

W8BCD

John M Poplin
1562 Rebecca Ann
El Paso TX 79936

KF5FTU
Ronald L Zerr
11225 Red Hawk Ln
El Paso TX 79936

WT5RZ
Ronald L Zerr
11225 Red Hawk Ln
El Paso TX 79936

W5FX
Michael D Bruening
415 Redd Rd 4B
El Paso TX 799321947

KC5DKC
Jaime G Nunez Cruz
210 Redd Rd Apt 116
El Paso TX 79932

AA5GH
Max Immerman
608 Regan St
El Paso TX 79903

KF5IWU
Sergio Benavides
10269 Renfrew Dr
El Paso TX 79925

WD9GCJ
Antonio Piccolo
11450 Rex Baxter Dr
El Paso TX 79936

KA5DKD
Johnny A Gooch
5753 Rick Husband Dr
El Paso TX 79934

N5OGJ
William J Deragisch
301 Ridgemont Dr
El Paso TX 79912

KA5VVN
James M Peterson
10244 Ridgewood
El Paso TX 79925

N8NBE
Michael J Hissam
712 Rinconada Ln
El Paso TX 79922

N5MQV
Arnoldo Osuna
405 Rio Arriba
El Paso TX 79907

KB5MQG
Luis Fierro Jr
3631 Rivera
El Paso TX 79905

KD6JFO
Derald H Smith
4520 Rj Lynn Ct
El Paso TX 79924

WB5TFT
Earl J Patin
9231 Roanoke Dr
El Paso TX 79924

KD5KZL
Joseph M Lorentzen
9506 Roanoke Dr
El Paso TX 79924

KB5KDP
Margarita V Serna
11012 Rockdale Dr
El Paso TX 79934

WB0HMV
Richard R Braun
5409 Rockwood Rd
El Paso TX 79932

WD0BAF
Dorothy A Braun
5409 Rockwood Rd
El Paso TX 79932

W5GYE
Jess Thurman
2909 Rocky Ridge
El Paso TX 79904

W5DNH
Roscoe O Little
2808 Rocky Ridge Dr
El Paso TX 79904

KE5ELR
Thomas E Conrow
14360 Roger Torres
El Paso TX 79938

KC5KJP
Pablo I Sanchez
1557A Rogers Rd
El Paso TX 79906

WA5DUX
James R Babington
4571 Rolling Stone
El Paso TX 79924

K5VRF
Robert C Smith
4700 Rolling Stone Ave
El Paso TX 799243032

KD5PTJ
William C Seigler
1632 Ronnie Reif Dr
El Paso TX 799365615

KE5ISU
Jeremy B Barrington
5544 Rosenstock St
El Paso TX 79906

KE5ELQ
Wayne W Braasch
4941 Round Rock Dr
El Paso TX 79924

KD6IQI
David A Scott
1421 Rudy Montoya
El Paso TX 79936

KD6IQH
Andrew T Scott
1421 Rudy Montoya
El Paso TX 799366845

KF5EIN
Marcel Kleinelsen
11615 Rufus Brijalba
El Paso TX 79936

W0RTS
George D Smarr
3722 Sacramento

El Paso TX 79930

W5JHS
John H Scheiderer
7206 Safford Ct
El Paso TX 79915

WB5HGL
Judith A Scheiderer
7206 Safford Ct
El Paso TX 799151366

KC5NLS
Kenneth S Koscielski
5053 Sagittarius
El Paso TX 79924

KC5YPC
Juan C Lozano
719 Saguaro Way
El Paso TX 799073616

WB5JXH
John T Bracey Sr
10288 Saigon Dr
El Paso TX 79925

KD5CMO
John T Bracey Jr
10288 Saigon Dr
El Paso TX 799255531

WP4LKA
Pablo M Diaz-Ramos
11612 Saint Thomas Way
El Paso TX 799362143

WL7AR
Cora L Worsham
5407 Salisbury
El Paso TX 79924

KD5GHL
Carlos Soto
11139 Sam Snead Dr
El Paso TX 79936

KC8EBM
Charles W Schroeder
452 San Blas
El Paso TX 79912

W5ES
 El Paso Amateur Radio Club

2100 San Diego Ave
El Paso TX 79930

KB5IOQ
Ben J Favela
2016 San Jose Ave
El Paso TX 79902

KB5FSQ
Charles S Von Sternberg
8017 San Jose Rd Apt 36 Bldg 2
El Paso TX 79915

KF5BPG
Charles S Von Sternberg
8017 San Jose Rd Apt 36 Bldg 2
El Paso TX 79915

N5GMS
Charles S Von Sternberg
8017 San Jose Rd Apt 36 Bldg 2
El Paso TX 79915

WD5CQL
William B Springer Jr
7129 San Marino
El Paso TX 79912

KE5FJL
Gordon R Couch
7137 San Marino
El Paso TX 79912

KE5UPE
Jackson M Vanderburg
7036 San Marino Dr
El Paso TX 79912

KB2SMA
James A Woodard
7137 San Marino Dr
El Paso TX 799121520

KB5RBD
Che M Trillo
2107 Sandiego
El Paso TX 79930

KA3LGB
Artis Wright
720 Santa Barbara Dr
El Paso TX 79915

KB5LCQ

Damajanti Widjaja
4300 Santa Rita
El Paso TX 79902

KA5OSX
Lonnie L Abernethy Jr
4301 Santa Rita
El Paso TX 79902

KB5EMI
Eva K Morgan
1728 Sara Rachel
El Paso TX 79927

W5TFT
William H Holcombe Jr
1941 Saul Kleinfeld 302
El Paso TX 79936

KG5XJ
Woodrow W Finch
1941 Saul Kleinfeld Apt 227
El Paso TX 79936

W5TGY
Evelyne Mc Laughlin
2500 Scenic Crest
El Paso TX 79930

KG4NKE
Matthew K Baptiste
5560 Schenck St
El Paso TX 79906

KG4NKF
Rosita Baptiste
5560 Schenck St
El Paso TX 79906

KD5LPP
Oscar Pilhoefer
3108 Sea Breeze
El Paso TX 79936

N5ZWX
Hendrik Aalderts
2521 Sea Palm
El Paso TX 79936

AE5OJ
Paul D Wilson
2516 Sea Palm Dr
El Paso TX 79936

KB5FQL
Robert D Stark
10456 Seawood
El Paso TX 79925

WB5GJK
Edward S Bashur II
10457 Seawood
El Paso TX 79925

WB5WIF
Sandra T Bashur
10457 Seawood
El Paso TX 799257821

KB5NBY
Ireneo G Banuelos
1203 Selden Dr
El Paso TX 79903

NP3AX
Leonard Padin Gonzalez
11432 Selma Ct
El Paso TX 79936

KE5OVS
David E Stewart
1309 Shadow Canyon
El Paso TX 79912

KE5ZMI
Sierra A Stewart
1309 Shadow Canyon
El Paso TX 79912

KE5ZMJ
Savanna R Stewart
1309 Shadow Canyon
El Paso TX 79912

WB5SCL
Francis B Gallagher
252 Shadow Mount Dr F9
El Paso TX 79912

KF6PVT
Andrew P Spencer
368 Shadow Mountain Dr 105C
El Paso TX 799124034

KA5IXK
Robert I Sinn
300 Shadow Mountain Dr 201
El Paso TX 79912

KD5UEK
Miguel A Nunez
2037 Shadow Ridge Dr
El Paso TX 79938

KE5APX
Warren G Beadle
9804 Sidewinder
El Paso TX 799244924

KD5GBN
Daniel Tarin
221 Siesta Way
El Paso TX 79922

KB5HTV
Goliath Martinez
4225 Siete Leguas
El Paso TX 79922

WA5ERX
Marcelo Salinas
10513 Sigma
El Paso TX 79924

WB5HPO
Lela H Wilson
2305 Silver Ave
El Paso TX 79930

KF5LRG
Jose O Santillan
3732 Silver Palm
El Paso TX 79936

KB5BSF
Robert L Lebkowsky
100A Silver Shadow Dr
El Paso TX 79912

N5WAX
Robert J Simpson
4030 Skyline
El Paso TX 79904

KT6S
Reginald C Sweet
4020 Skyline Ave
El Paso TX 79904

AB5FP
Lloyd K Mark
309 Skyway

El Paso TX 79912

K9CMU
Gerald H Klein
3405 Slocum St
El Paso TX 79936

N5OUL
Parke W Weidler
724 Somerset Dr
El Paso TX 79912

N5XRC
John M Worthy
725 Somerset Dr
El Paso TX 79912

KD5HLP
Humberto Montoya
9233 Sorbonne
El Paso TX 79907

KB5HUL
Jose L Atilano
316 South Concepcion
El Paso TX 79905

KB5HIA
Raquel S Grijalva
615 South El Paso Apt 17
El Paso TX 79901

KB5FZN
Mary Ruth Bedford
110 South Festival Dr Apt A5
El Paso TX 799125821

KA5VBT
Ricardo Vilardell
129 South Little Flower
El Paso TX 79915

KA5YIQ
Irma M Vilardell
129 South Little Flower
El Paso TX 79915

AB5OH
Donald A Kern Sr
611 South Val Verde St
El Paso TX 79905

W5NTI
James A Hiatt

1027 St Johns Dr
El Paso TX 799033312

KF5LPJ
Steven A Lozano
8110 Staghorn Dr
El Paso TX 79907

WA5RMH
Richard L Hayden
9404 Stahala Dr
El Paso TX 79924

KB5OLI
Robert J Witte
1005 Stanley St
El Paso TX 79907

K5FTE
Earl C Harris
1009 Stanley St
El Paso TX 799072331

K5JLE
Wayne L Miller
1231 Stockwell Ln
El Paso TX 79902

KB5DSM
Patrick M Strong
529 Stonebluff
El Paso TX 79912

KB5MGE
Mark D Novick
432 Stotts
El Paso TX 79932

KI5XG
Anthony I Gronich
448 Stotts
El Paso TX 79932

KK5FP
Richard B Novick
432 Stotts Ave
El Paso TX 79932

KK5TU
Guus J Kemmler
8919 Strand Ln
El Paso TX 79904

WA5YRP

Earl E Wood
8921 Strand Ln
El Paso TX 79904

KB5MMD
Ross K Brown
205 Stratus
El Paso TX 79912

KJ5WH
Mark E Duran
10161 Sumatra
El Paso TX 79925

KB5IUM
Robert W Blanchard
5824 Sun Court Cir
El Paso TX 79924

W5RGH
Richard G Harper
12413 Sun Terrace Ave
El Paso TX 79938

KE5ZEB
Adrian B Solano
12640 Sun Trl
El Paso TX 79938

WA5WPX
Ricardo R Perez
4736 Sun Valley Dr
El Paso TX 79924

KM5GU
Richard B Gregor
4939 Sun Valley Dr
El Paso TX 79924

KD5IPW
David T Denman
8820 Sunland Rd
El Paso TX 79907

N5QVE
Richard F Thrift
5820 Sunnyvale Cir
El Paso TX 79924

KD5EEC
Jeanne L Gregor
4939 Sunvalley
El Paso TX 79924

KB5HUJ
John E Weber
5773 Sweetwater
El Paso TX 79924

N5FHL
Hugh I Trotter Jr
5220 Sweetwater St
El Paso TX 79924

KE5ZMK
Nathan J Ashby
1117 Talon Pl
El Paso TX 79912

K5ED
Charles E Jensen
6424 Tarascas Dr
El Paso TX 79912

K5PUP
Isabel C Jensen
6424 Tarascas Dr
El Paso TX 79912

KB5NEP
Kyon L Patten
5800 Tautoga Dr
El Paso TX 79924

KA5RZD
Richard E Haynes Sr
3223 Taylor Ave
El Paso TX 79930

K5KDW
Mary J Willmon
3332 Taylor Ave
El Paso TX 79930

KE5OHZ
Mark L Yakubovsky
5840 Teal
El Paso TX 79924

W5YAK
Mark L Yakubovsky
5840 Teal
El Paso TX 79924

W5LYZ
Glenn E Mock
6127 Tejas Dr
El Paso TX 799052105

KB5IYK
Lanneau Golucke
11185 Tenaha
El Paso TX 79936

K5ITB
Benard Hirsh
643 Tepic Dr
El Paso TX 79912

KE5QLX
Robert C Evans
611 Tepic Rd
El Paso TX 79912

W5NDG
Edmund A Davis
11109 Terrell Ave
El Paso TX 79936

K5HPJ
Jon A White
6201 Tesuque Dr
El Paso TX 79905

KC5GEE
Rodolfo Borjon
4841 Tetons
El Paso TX 79904

KC5PUX
Roger U Poerce
4733 Tetons Dr
El Paso TX 799042818

KB5IUN
Victor Vega
210 Thomas
El Paso TX 79915

KC7UXM
Craig A Lyles
10317 Thor St
El Paso TX 79924

KE5CXB
Danielle E Robinson
5134 Thornton
El Paso TX 79932

KD5SWB
Esther M Robinson
5134 Thornton

El Paso TX 799322541

KF5CMW
Tirzah A Robinson
5134 Thornton St
El Paso TX 79932

K3FQE
Hadley Robinson
5134 Thornton St
El Paso TX 799322541

KC5FGA
Nathan H Robinson
5134 Thornton St
El Paso TX 799322541

KC5LPV
Anna R Robinson
5134 Thornton St
El Paso TX 799322541

N5HWB
Marilyn E Robinson
5134 Thornton St
El Paso TX 799322541

N5LGE
Shiloah D Warren
350 Thunderbird 42
El Paso TX 79912

N5LOE
John M Warren
350 Thunderbird 42
El Paso TX 79912

KA5MGA
William H Courson
1088 Thunderbird Dr
El Paso TX 79912

K5HJZ
Betty L Mac Guire
1209 Thunderbird Dr
El Paso TX 79912

K5HLC
John T Mac Guire
1209 Thunderbird Dr
El Paso TX 79912

KF5JHH
James A Cox

1217 Thunderbird Dr
El Paso TX 79912

NE8U
James A Cox
1217 Thunderbird Dr
El Paso TX 79912

KC5DKB
Yvonne Jaurigue
10604 Tiber Pl
El Paso TX 79924

KF5IWV
Monica Ortega
12704 Tierra Alexis
El Paso TX 79938

KC6WWR
Eugene Rangel Jr
12348 Tierra Arroyo Dr
El Paso TX 79938

KE5UOX
Eduardo Delgadillo
12365 Tierra Canada
El Paso TX 79938

N5ZRE
Richard Crespo
12329 Tierra Laurel
El Paso TX 79938

KF5NHG
Preston D Ramos
12236 Tierra Maya Dr
El Paso TX 79938

KG6MUG
Mark P Leahy
12448 Tierra Nogal Dr
El Paso TX 79938

N5WPV
Arthur R Smith Sr
3060 Tierra Nora Dr
El Paso TX 79938

KC5LPR
Tom R Wuerschmidt
5516 Timberwolf
El Paso TX 79903

KE5AXX

Mary L Wuerschmidt
5516 Timberwolf
El Paso TX 79903

KA5EWK
Robert D Schoen
9849 Titan
El Paso TX 79924

KB5VEK
James O Hargrove
9912 Titan St
El Paso TX 79924

K5DIT
Edmund B Corliss Sr
3623 Titanic
El Paso TX 79904

N5XNG
David E Hennis
3228 Titanic Ave
El Paso TX 79904

KE5UDO
Isabel Vargas
4636 Titanic Ave
El Paso TX 79904

K5YH
Francis L Bennett
3229 Titanic Dr
El Paso TX 79904

KF5GQF
Hans F Muller
13191 Tobacco Rd
El Paso TX 79938

W5HFN
Hans F Muller
13191 Tobacco Rd
El Paso TX 79938

K5AP
Harold H Bernhard
113 Tobar Way
El Paso TX 79912

KD5MEQ
Paige M Stripling
6805 Toluca
El Paso TX 79912

WB5QLR
Thomas C Stripling
6805 Toluca
El Paso TX 79912

K5IJB
Lawrence C Nelson Jr
7005 Toluca
El Paso TX 799121518

WA5MHE
Lawrence C Nelson Jr
7005 Toluca
El Paso TX 799121518

KA5HPI
Cheri S Dotson
1816 Tommy Aaron
El Paso TX 79936

KD5BVL
Daniel Beltran
1816 Tommy Aaron
El Paso TX 79936

N5ONY
Jasper W Dotson
1816 Tommy Aaron
El Paso TX 79936

N5BHR
James J Phillips
1645 Tommy Aaron Dr
El Paso TX 79936

KC5EEK
John W Saunders
1716 Tommy Aaron Dr
El Paso TX 79936

W8OSD
Virginia S Thompson
10528 Tomwood Ave
El Paso TX 79925

WB5ILK
Wallace T Thompson
10528 Tomwood Ave
El Paso TX 799257812

K5YHZ
Kenneth M Pearsall
11628 Tony Tejeda Dr
El Paso TX 79936

KD5YBG
Dale R Colburn
10816 Tourmaline
El Paso TX 79924

KE6MYJ
Dale R Colburn
10816 Tourmaline
El Paso TX 79924

KC5FIN
Roger D Graham
5301 Transmountain 1101
El Paso TX 79924

K5JFV
Richard A Zubiate
2125 Tremont St
El Paso TX 79930

KB5YVG
Gloria O Ivey
11632 Trey Burton
El Paso TX 79936

WD5KBC
Bobby C Moon
10445 Triumph Dr
El Paso TX 79924

KC5FFU
Richard L Wineman
5736 Tropacina St
El Paso TX 79924

WB5VMI
Diane L Mc Mellen
5012 Tropicana
El Paso TX 79924

WA5HLO
Derrell R Bearden
4628 Tropicana Ave
El Paso TX 79924

WB5RVL
Irene A Bearden
4628 Tropicana Ave
El Paso TX 79924

K5YIE
Charles L Benzinger
3406 Truman

El Paso TX 79930

KE5ZMN
Samuel Alva
4418 Tularosa Ave
El Paso TX 79903

KC5KNR
Charles L Vanderveer
4800 Tumbleweed Ave
El Paso TX 79924

WB5KND
James P Bush
4710 Turf 12
El Paso TX 799389709

KC5JFG
William M Edsall Jr
4477 Turf Rd
El Paso TX 79938

WB5UNG
Mary H Bush
4710 Turf Sp 12
El Paso TX 79938

KF4MIS
Eric E Sifford
12725 Tuscan Hills Ct
El Paso TX 799384384

N5HVX
Ramiro Zaldivar
10112 Tuscany
El Paso TX 79924

WB5VPT
John R Simon
1540 Upson Dr
El Paso TX 79902

W5MQA
Pete E M Warren III
6200 Valeria
El Paso TX 79912

KD6CHR
Isidro R Enriquez
11420 Valle Grande
El Paso TX 79927

N5DRE
Wesley H Bopp

8178 Valley View
El Paso TX 79907

KF5IGP
Darwin E Hall
3520 Van Buren Ave
El Paso TX 79930

W5HTH
James M Hardison
3808 Vega Ct
El Paso TX 79904

KE5JOM
Matthew T Usevitch
851 Via Corta
El Paso TX 79912

KE5JON
David E Usevitch
851 Via Corta
El Paso TX 79912

KE5JOO
James B Usevitch
851 Via Corta
El Paso TX 79912

KC5SJM
Thomas G Carranza
12263 Via Del Rio
El Paso TX 799366474

N5PIX
Christos E Maragoudakis
913 Via Norte Ln
El Paso TX 79912

KC5MNZ
Joe S Friedel
5913 Via Robles
El Paso TX 79912

W5GYZ
Joe S Friedel
5913 Via Robles
El Paso TX 79912

KE5ZMW
Jamison B Moody
6052 Via Serena Dr
El Paso TX 79912

KE5ZMX

Christian T Moody
6052 Via Serena Dr
El Paso TX 79912

KE5ZMY
Jamison M Moody
6052 Via Serena Dr
El Paso TX 79912

N5ZRG
David F Palyu
5221 Viceroy Dr
El Paso TX 79924

WA5MGP
Donald E Evans Sr
9107 Vicksburg
El Paso TX 79924

KC5FIJ
Howard S Hancock
9201 Vicksburg
El Paso TX 79924

KE5BHU
Cherry M Smith
9529 Vicksburg Dr
El Paso TX 79924

KA5CDJ
Thomas B Smith
9529 Vicksburg Dr
El Paso TX 799246213

W5DPD
Cherry M Smith
9529 Vicksburg Dr
El Paso TX 799246213

KD5CLW
Joseluis Espinosa
1632 Victor Lopez
El Paso TX 79936

KA5NCO
Buena T Milson
252 Viking
El Paso TX 79912

WA5AAQ
James L Milson
252 Viking Dr
El Paso TX 79912

KD5PLC
Charlotte E Yates
732 Villa Flores
El Paso TX 79912

KF5DGU
Marissa L Pazos
6757 Villa Hermosa
El Paso TX 79912

N0QAC
Michael G Maurer
6807 Villa Hermosa Dr
El Paso TX 799122328

KF5LUN
Joseph P O'Connor
12050 Village Gate Dr
El Paso TX 79936

KD5RSH
Bodo Geue
9455 Viscount 156
El Paso TX 79925

WA5BGG
Candelario B Aguilar
9455 Viscount Apt 524
El Paso TX 79925

KG4FBY
David A Cunningham
8855 Viscount Blvd 441
El Paso TX 79925

KE5WHL
Daniel D Paton
9353 Viscount Blvd Apt 1075
El Paso TX 79925

KB1HRS
Michael J Lynch
9375 Viscount Blvd Apt 903
El Paso TX 799258083

KB5WHO
Paul L Forhan
10624 Vista Alegre
El Paso TX 79935

KC5RGP
Rita L Forhan
10624 Vista Alegre Dr
El Paso TX 79935

KB5SQE
Douglas L Craft
1212 Vista De Oro D
El Paso TX 79935

W6AKP
Robert M Young
265 Vista Del Rey
El Paso TX 79912

KF5OLQ
Mercedes M De La Rosa
10816 Vista Lomas Dr
El Paso TX 79935

KC5JOR
Henry Campbell
1636 Vista Real
El Paso TX 79935

KC5JOS
Laura V Campbell
1636 Vista Real
El Paso TX 79935

N5EP
 El Paso Contest Club
3109 Vogue Dr
El Paso TX 79935

KB5QZT
William W Childress
11156 Volare Dr
El Paso TX 79936

N5EJI
Harold V Leininger
3200 Voss Dr
El Paso TX 79936

N5PAW
Antonio G Duque
3229 Voss Dr
El Paso TX 79936

KA5GYY
Gaylon E Peterson
5713 Waldorf Dr
El Paso TX 79924

N2OYY
Owen Moore
5741 Waldorf Dr

El Paso TX 79924

KB5HPS
Enrique Perlasca
200 Wallington 235
El Paso TX 79902

KF5AZS
Jerald J Brady III
200 Wallington Dr Apt 69
El Paso TX 79902

KB5LSJ
Jason E Abbott
10537 Warren
El Paso TX 79924

KB5IUK
Pedro F Zenker
3221 Wayside
El Paso TX 79936

N6OMY
Claud L Drennan III
3220 Wedgewood
El Paso TX 79925

N6XKQ
M Zita Drennan
3220 Wedgewood
El Paso TX 79925

KB5JJX
William M Reves
3327 Wedgewood
El Paso TX 79925

KD5FMV
Cassandra S Hoshor
4141 West City Ct 114
El Paso TX 79902

W5MVL
Wilbur T Mcgill
8800 West H Burges Dr
El Paso TX 79902

KD5TAB
Maki Kirita
600 West Paisano
El Paso TX 79901

KD5SGW
Yu-Sheng Chang

600 West Paisano Dr
El Paso TX 79901

KE5AHX
Randy S Hagood
415 West Redd Rd - 21A
El Paso TX 79932

KD5JAF
Alfonso Meneses
100 West Robinson D-3
El Paso TX 79902

KB5LXU
Valentine O Hahn
5528 Westside Dr 1
El Paso TX 79932

KC5UPI
Dale L Adair
3306 Wexford
El Paso TX 79925

KD5CEC
Marguerite D Adair
3306 Wexford
El Paso TX 79925

KE5COJ
Jack C Hart
11140 Wharf Cove
El Paso TX 79936

AA5AP
Clayton B Hamilton
11184 Wharf Cove
El Paso TX 79936

KC5WPH
Federico D Marin
6870 Whisper Canyon
El Paso TX 799127443

KA5SZB
Josephine B Mc Carty
5302 Whispering Wind
El Paso TX 79936

NO5A
Edwin L Mc Carty
5302 Whispering Wind Dr
El Paso TX 79936

KA6CLF

Louise M Powell
5200 White Oak Dr
El Paso TX 79932

KE5ZMU
Gary W Cadd
10745 White Sands
El Paso TX 79924

W5QZS
Charles R Landers
11024 Whitehall Dr
El Paso TX 79934

KD5EUB
Lindy C Patterson
10219 Whitetail
El Paso TX 79924

KD5APZ
Raymond E Branham
3612 Wickham
El Paso TX 79904

KM5HS
Monroe H Shelton III
3633 Wickham Ave
El Paso TX 79904

K5KKO
El Paso Digital Intertie Group
3709 Wickham Ave
El Paso TX 79904

KD5NWM
El Paso Skywarn
3709 Wickham Ave
El Paso TX 79904

KD5ZDP
El Paso Digital Intertie Group
3709 Wickham Ave
El Paso TX 79904

WX5ELP
El Paso Skywarn
3709 Wickham Ave
El Paso TX 79904

K5WPH
Sun City Amateur Radio Club
Inc
3709 Wickham St
El Paso TX 79904

KF5FOU
Kevin A Dorman
5757 Will Ruth Apt 114
El Paso TX 79924

KE5ZMP
Matthew P Smith
6586 Wind Ridge
El Paso TX 79912

W1HX
Norman H Young
7348 Wind Song Dr
El Paso TX 79912

W1NUO
Tisha L Young
7348 Wind Song Dr
El Paso TX 79912

KB5HTF
David P Hensgen
2109 Windrock
El Paso TX 79925

KD5QNI
Jose Ontiveros Jr
10112 Wolverine
El Paso TX 79924

KE5FYD
Jariell Alexis Perlman
10325 Woodard Ct
El Paso TX 79925

KE5GUW
Sean C O'Beirne
2124 Woodside Dr
El Paso TX 79925

KE5GUY
John J O'Beirne
2124 Woodside Dr
El Paso TX 79925

KE5RSI
Michael Joiner
5249 Wren Ave 133
El Paso TX 79924

KB5HXI
Salvador Espinoza Jr
1221 Wyoming

El Paso TX 79902

KB5HXQ
George Natividad
4406 Wyoming
El Paso TX 79903

KB5UDD
Ruben Montiel
1220 Wyoming St
El Paso TX 79902

KB5KYE
Patrick M Denney
2809 Yarbrough 1
El Paso TX 79925

KB5ZHK
Hector G Olvera
2655 Yarbrough 139
El Paso TX 79925

KC5HFF
Miles A Jackson
4501 Yulcan 138
El Paso TX 79904

WB9TEV
Daniel D Pipes
1328 Yvonne Diane Dr
El Paso TX 799357415

KK5NH
Joyce A Posey
3334 Zion J3
El Paso TX 79904

KE5QS
Laura M Nicholson
El Paso TX 79902

N5DRZ
Fred J Mc Clain
El Paso TX 79902

N5FFB
Maureen B Mc Clain
El Paso TX 79902

KE5KVG
L W Brannon
El Paso TX 79904

KF5CJP

Heinz-Ulrich U Landeck
El Paso TX 79904

KF5KBR
Winston A Holmes
El Paso TX 79906

NL7ZL
Thomas L Robertson
El Paso TX 79906

KA5TWN
Jack E Yeager
El Paso TX 79913

KE5ZD
Harold R Loftus
El Paso TX 79914

KF5GQI
Eric Romero
El Paso TX 79917

KC5EJ
Franklin R Fultz
El Paso TX 79923

KD5KFY
Artis Wright
El Paso TX 79926

K5ELP
West Texas Repeater Assn
El Paso TX 79931

AB5ZK
Nelson P Smith
El Paso TX 79954

KD5CSZ
Hans Juergen Rache
El Paso TX 79982

W5BQU
Byrl H Burdick Sr
El Paso TX 79995

K5KWK
Kenneth W Kuhblank Jr
El Paso TX 79996

KF5EWU
Robert T Hercules
El Paso TX 79997

KF5HXD
Guillermo C Esparza III
El Paso TX 79997

KV5ROB
Robert T Hercules
El Paso TX 79997

K6RSX
Desmond G Boyle
El Paso TX 799132061

K0EOS
James P Rutledge
El Paso TX 799132361

AC5QS
Ed M Beeler
El Paso TX 799370636

KC5CET
Robert M Hafele
El Paso TX 79904

KB5UDA
Jackson L Rose Jr
El Paso TX 79913

KB5HAF
Dennis R Wagner
El Paso TX 79914

W4MAT
Sidney M Bedford Jr
El Paso TX 79952

FCC Amateur Radio Licenses in Fabens

WB2SDG
Allen Mower
134 East Annora Ave
Fabens TX 79838

KF5CJO
Stephen J Conjulusa
Fabens TX 79838

KF5CJQ
Mark V Conlon
Fabens TX 79838

KF5DJP

Denise V Conlon
Fabens TX 79838

W5DZM
Denise V Conlon
Fabens TX 79838

W5MZD
Mark V Conlon
Fabens TX 79838

KB5HPY
Pedro Hernandez
Fabens TX 79838

WB5HGK
Fred J Schuller
Fabens TX 79838

FCC Amateur Radio Licenses in Fort Bliss

KC5BUP
Cameron Brown
Box 3130
Fort Bliss TX 79916

KD5BSV
Michael A Brown
1 Ada
Fort Bliss TX 79916

KC5JFH
William D Searuggs
1924A Austin Rd
Fort Bliss TX 79906

KB5VCU
Rodney L Young
6341C Berry Cir
Fort Bliss TX 79916

KB5YVH
Michael W Bester
2207A McCullough
Fort Bliss TX 79906

N5UYQ
David L Eberhardt
5246A Montague Lp
Fort Bliss TX 79906

W8OAJ
Orville A Jones

201 Sheridan
Fort Bliss TX 79916

N7OEJ
Mickey K Mullikin
9338B Somerville
Fort Bliss TX 79906

AB5FX
Arden J Tefft
Fort Bliss TX 79906

FCC Amateur Radio Licenses in Fort Davis

K7TTF
Jerald S Morris
107 Antler Dr
Fort Davis TX 797342502

K5TDA
Terry D Allison
208 Apache Mountain Trl
Fort Davis TX 79734

K5ITT
Kitty J Sibayan
208 Apache Mountain Trl
Fort Davis TX 79734

KE5RAQ
Kitty J Sibayan
208 Apache Mountain Trl
Fort Davis TX 79734

KA5IYW
Clement S Boulter Jr
HCR 74 Box 152
Fort Davis TX 79734

AD5OF
Paul C Griebenow
HCR 74 Box 17
Fort Davis TX 79734

KD5VUB
Paul C Griebenow
HCR 74 Box 17
Fort Davis TX 79734

KD5OJM
Price B Middlebrook III
HC 75 Box 178
Fort Davis TX 797349801

KD5YBQ
William T Largent
HCR 74 Box 20
Fort Davis TX 79734

K5EGF
David F Klassen
HCR 74 Box 30
Fort Davis TX 79734

KC5RBB
Glenda H Klassen
HCR 74 Box 30
Fort Davis TX 79734

KE5ATV
Timothy R Caswell
HC 75 Box 410
Fort Davis TX 79734

AD5OH
Jonathan O Baize
HCR 74 Box 53
Fort Davis TX 79734

AD5OJ
Jonathan O Baize
HCR 74 Box 53
Fort Davis TX 79734

KD5VUC
William W Baize
HCR 74 Box 53
Fort Davis TX 79734

KD5VUD
Jonathan O Baize
HCR 74 Box 53
Fort Davis TX 79734

KE5ATW
Charles M Baize
HCR 74 Box 53
Fort Davis TX 79734

W7DIO
Ernest G Fairbank
Rt 1 Box 70
Fort Davis TX 79734

W5DBF
Clement S Boulter Jr
101 Broken Arrow Tr

Fort Davis TX 79734

KF5IYP
Robert H Newman
100 Cedar Ct
Fort Davis TX 79734

W5RHN
Robert H Newman
100 Cedar Ct
Fort Davis TX 79734

N5VGW
Catherine Gossett
104 Century Ln Hc 75 Box 188
Fort Davis TX 79734

KI5ZQ
Kenneth W Gossett
104 Century Ln Hc75 Box 188
Fort Davis TX 79734

KF5KLZ
Larry J Sheffield
205 Dave St
Fort Davis TX 79734

WB5BSB
W Allen Gilchrist Jr
104 Deer Ridge Dr
Fort Davis TX 79734

WB5YFG
John P Schwartz
104 Lt Gibbons
Fort Davis TX 79734

KF5ETA
Judith S Meyer
3 Lunar Landing
Fort Davis TX 79734

KF5ETB
Kevin R Meyer
3 Lunar Landing
Fort Davis TX 79734

KF5HBO
Judith S Meyer
3 Lunar Landing
Fort Davis TX 79734

KF5HBP
Kevin R Meyer

3 Lunar Landing
Fort Davis TX 79734

KB5YVJ
David R Doss
Mc Donald Observatory
Fort Davis TX 79734

KA5YPW
Sandra A Billingsley
403 Sgt Mulhern Loop
Fort Davis TX 79734

N5HXZ
Stewart Billingsley
403 Sgt Mulhern Loop
Fort Davis TX 79734

KF5JWO
Bruce D Bates Jr
102 Squaw Valle Trl
Fort Davis TX 79734

KF5KFK
Bruce D Bates Jr
102 Squaw Valle Trl
Fort Davis TX 79734

N5BBJ
Bruce D Bates Jr
102 Squaw Valley Trl
Fort Davis TX 79734

WA5AUR
Howard G Johnson Jr
42617 State Hwy 118
Fort Davis TX 797342517

KC5RHU
Bruce W Burkman
200 State St South
Fort Davis TX 79734

KA3ZOO
William L Zoulek
Fort Davis TX 79734

KC5NSB
Edna M Zoulek
Fort Davis TX 79734

KD5EFY
Kevin L Ernhart
Fort Davis TX 79734

KD5FYN
Rodney R Barrick
Fort Davis TX 79734

KD5KBU
James R Fowler
Fort Davis TX 79734

KD5SKZ
Jesse D Stark
Fort Davis TX 79734

KE5MKL
Joshua D Fowler
Fort Davis TX 79734

N5HYD
Douglas S Otoupal
Fort Davis TX 79734

N5MVV
Angie Otoupal
Fort Davis TX 79734

KB5EDS
Jess Whitfield
Fort Davis TX 79734

KC5EYP
Robert T Wooster Sr
Fort Davis TX 79734

KC5FNC
Camille D Doss
Fort Davis TX 79734

KM5V
Vicki L Riley
Fort Davis TX 79734

FCC Amateur Radio Licenses in Fort Hancock

KC5LPT
Joel A Bishop
HCR 66 Box 35
Fort Hancock TX 79839

KB5ESA
Irma K Cook
Fort Hancock TX 79839

FCC Amateur Radio Licenses in Fort Stockton

KC5QCA
Stacy A Mc Collom
Box 1177
Fort Stockton TX 79735

KB5JXO
Benny Walker Jr
Box 359
Fort Stockton TX 79735

KA5JIU
Neva G Mc Corkle
Box 422
Fort Stockton TX 797350422

KA5INY
Patricia M Slack
Rt 1 Box 61B Imperial Hwy
Fort Stockton TX 79735

N5LKY
Bonnie J Warnock
Rt 1 Box 81
Fort Stockton TX 79735

KB5DXM
Frederick H Prano
418 East 10th St
Fort Stockton TX 79735

WB5HHZ
John E Cope
707 East 11th
Fort Stockton TX 79735

N5OJL
Connie L Parks
1448 East 48th
Fort Stockton TX 79735

N5LKZ
Lonnie D Parks
1398 East 48th Ln
Fort Stockton TX 79735

N5LKX
Ronnie L Parks
1448 East 48th Ln
Fort Stockton TX 79735

KC5SLN

Lorenzo Mercado
504 East Gonzalez Rd
Fort Stockton TX 79735

N5LIR
Emery R Strother Jr
1603 North Gillis
Fort Stockton TX 79735

WB5FWR
Albert E Bean
706 North Missouri St
Fort Stockton TX 79735

KA5KPH
Ray S Martinez
1507 North Nelson
Fort Stockton TX 79735

KB5JYT
Ray R Martinez
1507 North Nelson
Fort Stockton TX 79735

KB5JYU
Naomi C Martinez
1507 North Nelson
Fort Stockton TX 79735

KB5JXQ
Kelly C Bryant
406 North Pecos Box 1302
Fort Stockton TX 79735

KF5AEJ
Robbie A Dominguez
1100 North Schlegel St
Fort Stockton TX 79735

KE5OCM
Lucia A Gilbert
606 North Texas
Fort Stockton TX 79735

WB5WSX
Stanley Phillips
1801 North Texas
Fort Stockton TX 79735

KE5MSQ
Harold D Bonham
5129 North Wilson Way
Fort Stockton TX 79735

KC5KZN
Loraine W Lannom
P O Box 1182
Fort Stockton TX 79735

N5LZW
Mabel F Bortner
Parkview Mobile Home Park
Fort Stockton TX 79735

KB5JXP
Jeffery D Bryant
406 Pecos St
Fort Stockton TX 79735

N5DLX
Richard W Mc Gee
101 Sage St
Fort Stockton TX 79735

N5NAM
James M Shelton
301 South Colpitts
Fort Stockton TX 79735

KF5MJN
Joshua R Ureta
103 South Hadden
Fort Stockton TX 79735

N5LOM
Carrie L Norton
103 South Mendel
Fort Stockton TX 79735

NN5DX
Ronald J Marosko Jr
304 South Mesquite St
Fort Stockton TX 79735

KE5MSR
Sean M Kneuper
302 South Missouri
Fort Stockton TX 79735

WB5NED
Felix E Kneuper
302 South Missouri
Fort Stockton TX 79735

WA5VMY
Ennis S Morgan
104 South Oklahoma St
Fort Stockton TX 79735

KF5MJM
Braydon K Moore
207 South Seals
Fort Stockton TX 79735

KC5GZN
Thomas C Hamilton
1703 West 1st St
Fort Stockton TX 797356304

WB5ARJ
Robert D Kresta
1812 West 8th
Fort Stockton TX 79735

KE5MSS
David L Mcmasters
1814 West 9th St
Fort Stockton TX 79735

N5PBV
Cheryl A Hailes
1702 West Callaghan
Fort Stockton TX 79735

KF5PEJ
Darren A Hodges
1904 West Callaghan St
Fort Stockton TX 79735

KE5AWT
Wireless Frontier Internet
Amateur Radio Club
1108 West Dickinson Blvd
Fort Stockton TX 79735

WI5FI
Wireless Frontier Internet
Amateur Radio Club
1108 West Dickinson Blvd
Fort Stockton TX 79735

W5GVQ
Martin L H Baze Jr
1607 West Division
Fort Stockton TX 79735

KB5GLA
Donald R Lannom
Fort Stockton TX 79735

KB5GLD
John D Mc Intyre

Fort Stockton TX 79735

KB5QKT
Dempsey G Wilson
Fort Stockton TX 79735

KE5MST
Colby M Cox
Fort Stockton TX 79735

KG5WS
Richard C Bortner
Fort Stockton TX 79735

N5BPJ
Patricia H Cox
Fort Stockton TX 79735

N5MXG
Cord Murphy
Fort Stockton TX 79735

WD5CGL
Charles F Cox
Fort Stockton TX 79735

KE5OCN
Sarah A Barnette
Fort Stockton TX 79735

KA5ICL
George R Mc Corkle
Fort Stockton TX 797350422

W5BQZ
Joe C Hallford Jr
Fort Stockton TX 797351454

KB5GLF
Joseph W Faubion Jr
Fort Stockton TX 79735

KB5GLH
Greg Murphy
Fort Stockton TX 79735

KB5GLI
Nathan W Wilcox
Fort Stockton TX 79735

KB5MMV
Stanley L Puckett
Fort Stockton TX 79735

N5LLQ
Charles E Jones
Fort Stockton TX 79735

N5MXF
Joseph W Faubion Sr
Fort Stockton TX 79735

N5ZJU
Jim Ed M Cope
Fort Stockton TX 79735

W5IKU
Billy F Coates
Fort Stockton TX 79735

WB5OTC
Robert G Barr
Fort Stockton TX 79735

FCC Amateur Radio Licenses in Gardendale

N5LTS
Adah L Ray
101 Dahlia
Gardendale TX 79758

KE5ATT
Gregg Bowington
3845 East Buttercup Dr
Gardendale TX 79758

KB5YYC
Jerry D Wiley
16356 Hollyhock
Gardendale TX 797580212

KE5LUZ
 Consortium Of Amateur Radio
Experimenters (Care)
16060 North Dale Wade Ave
Gardendale TX 79758

KE5LVA
 Motorola Amateur Radio Club
Of West Texas (Marc Wtx)
16060 North Dale Wade Ave
Gardendale TX 79758

WD5MOT
 Motorola Amateur Radio Club
Of West Texas (Marc Wtx)
16060 North Dale Wade Ave

Gardendale TX 79758

WR5FM
 Consortium Of Amateur Radio
Experimenters (Care)
16060 North Dale Wade Ave
Gardendale TX 79758

WV6H
Stuart M Hacken
16060 North Dale Wade Ave
Gardendale TX 797584310

KI6HJU
Paul A Nielsen
14630 North Hollyhock Ave 3
Gardendale TX 75758

KB5THR
Jerry W Naylor
14630 North Hollyhock Sp7
Gardendale TX 797584727

N7AXT
Nathan T Roberts
14049 North Midway Ave
Gardendale TX 79758

KF5LQQ
Melvin A Hill
16085 North Sunflower Ave
Gardendale TX 79758

N5RDQ
Danny Woodard
Gardendale TX 79758

KB5VGI
Barbara A Woodard
Gardendale TX 79758

FCC Amateur Radio Licenses in Grandfalls

WD5AEK
Richard D Hamm
207 1/2 Ave Box 248
Grandfalls TX 79742

FCC Amateur Radio Licenses in Horizon City

KA9DNO
Peter M Calvagna

14025 Desert Lily Pl
Horizon City TX 79928

WI9K
Wendy J Calvagna
14025 Desert Lily Pl
Horizon City TX 79928

W0PD
Michael G Mcconnell Sr
448 Desert Song Dr
Horizon City TX 79928

W0PDX
Carmen R Mcconnell
448 Desert Song Dr
Horizon City TX 79928

KA9VHY
Benjamin S Morales
14876 Kingston
Horizon City TX 79928

N2JKW
Javier Maldonado
101 Lago Grande
Horizon City TX 79928

K2GUY
Guy C Barber
13900 Pete La Rue
Horizon City TX 79928

KE5TFX
Guy C Barber
13900 Pete La Rue
Horizon City TX 79928

KD5HJE
Jesus J Camarillo
701 Plazer
Horizon City TX 79927

KD5FMZ
E Hubert Ruble
3710 Scobey Dr
Horizon City TX 799276930

FCC Amateur Radio Licenses in Imperial

KE5OCO
Shanna K Worthington
Imperial TX 79743

WA2YNE
Wayne C Leake
Imperial TX 79743

KB5GLJ
Melvin E Williams
Imperial TX 79743

KB5GLK
Lynda B Williams
Imperial TX 79743

FCC Amateur Radio Licenses in Iraan

W5NQZ
Stephen R Radway
304 West 3rd St
Iraan TX 79744

KF5AEK
Joe C Leyva
Iraan TX 79744

FCC Amateur Radio Licenses in Kent

N5PDY
Cliff J Teinert
 Box 3057
Kent TX 79855

FCC Amateur Radio Licenses in Kermit

W6CIH
William P Powers
1061 Adams St
Kermit TX 79745

KA5TRA
Melvin L Mayer
336 Bert St
Kermit TX 79745

KC5MDJ
Shauna S Gordon
901 East Waco
Kermit TX 79745

KC5MDK
Carl S Gordon
901 East Waco

Kermit TX 79745

N5IDL
Dillard W Barrick
1786 Halley St
Kermit TX 79745

KC5UXU
David A Smith
743 North Ash St
Kermit TX 79745

W5FLA
Claude B Smith
743 North Ash St
Kermit TX 79745

AC5WI
George W Merrell
618 North Ave C
Kermit TX 79745

KM5RE
George W Merrell
618 North Ave C
Kermit TX 79745

KF5LHK
Royce W Senn Jr
742 North Cedar
Kermit TX 79745

KE5MKG
Ruby J Garcia
200 South East Ave Apt 17
Kermit TX 79745

WB5ZAN
Larry K Potter
 SR Box 227
Kermit TX 79745

KB5MIH
Leonard T Shropshire
842 Underwood
Kermit TX 79745

W5VVF
Johnny B Walton
Kermit TX 79745

WB5QWB
Virginia R Godwin
Kermit TX 79745

FCC Amateur Radio Licenses in Marathon

KB5RCK
Charles M Sansom
309 North East 5th St
Marathon TX 79842

KB5LMB
Susan M Roberts
Marathon TX 79842

FCC Amateur Radio Licenses in Marfa

K5QPW
J Alfred Roosevelt
Bldg 98 Fort Russell Bx F
Marfa TX 79843

N2VZE
Philip H Davis
1999 Golf Course Rd
Marfa TX 79843

KD5EFX
Stanley J Dempsey
520 North Austin St
Marfa TX 798430487

W5TEH
Vernon L Rosson
900 West 2nd St
Marfa TX 798431533

KG5WT
Roger L Amis
418 West Texas
Marfa TX 79843

KA5UGF
Gary L Oliver
Marfa TX 79843

N5DCZ
Robert L Mann
Marfa TX 79843

FCC Amateur Radio Licenses in Mc Camey

W5YIN
Leonard L Rose

101 14th
McCamey TX 79752

KE5UAL
John M Babb
McCamey TX 79752

W5YIO
Virginia W Rose
McCamey TX 79752

KE5WZI
Carlota Babb
McCamey TX 79752

FCC Amateur Radio Licenses in Mc Donald Observatory

NW5M
Michael H Ward
13 Milky Way
McDonald Observatory TX
79734

K5WWR
Randall L Bryant
57 Mount Locke Rd E
McDonald Observatory TX
79734

KF5MPJ
Randall L Bryant
57 Mount Locke Rd E
McDonald Observatory TX
79734

FCC Amateur Radio Licenses in Mentone

KE5UAD
Harlan B Hopper
Mentone TX 79754

FCC Amateur Radio Licenses in Midland

W5QGR
Howell R Epps
123 Abell Hanger Cir
Midland TX 797076111

KK5MV
James D Reynolds
6005 Allandale Ct

Midland TX 79707

KC5ALI
Michael S Soper
907 Almont Pl
Midland TX 79705

KE5ZLC
Pok Duk Kim
908 Almont Pl
Midland TX 79705

KC5KFY
Thomas J La Farelle
3701 Amelia
Midland TX 79703

KC5KPY
Robert V Lafarelle
3701 Amelia
Midland TX 79703

KC5KFW
Michael F La Farelle
3701 Amelia St
Midland TX 74703

KB5ELQ
Steven S Power
700 Andrews Hwy
Midland TX 79703

KE5JZU
Justin W Kershner
4604 Anetta Dr
Midland TX 79703

KC5BQH
Justin A Burris
5108 Anetta Dr
Midland TX 79703

KB5SKX
David A Bell
4607 Aspen
Midland TX 79707

KB5JUZ
Roger D Vester
2812 Auburn
Midland TX 79705

KF5NFR
Michael E Cralle

2304 Auburn Pl
Midland TX 79705

KD5WKZ
Jose A Mallen
300 Baird St
Midland TX 79701

WB5C
Phil D Wilson
3316 Bedford
Midland TX 79703

KC5YFI
Beppe Niccolini
3400 Bedford
Midland TX 79703

N7OV
Oreste Venier
3400 Bedford
Midland TX 79703

WF5E
Leslie A Bannon
3400 Bedford
Midland TX 79703

KD5UVH
Steven R Niblett
5111 Belaire Dr
Midland TX 79703

KD5HCQ
Hunter M Watkins
4812 Bishops Castle
Midland TX 797051504

KF5KCJ
Marshall M Hughes
201 Blackberry
Midland TX 79705

WA7ISZ
Raymond M Heath
2805 Bluebird Ln
Midland TX 797052401

KG5ZA
John K Peterson
4700 Boulder 1105
Midland TX 797073302

KD5NSB

Troy L Rich
4700 Boulder 206
Midland TX 79707

KC5WUP
Robert L Wands
4725 Bowie Rd
Midland TX 79703

N5BKT
Banks Campbell
 Box 2034
Midland TX 79702

WA5BYH
W G Hadley
HC 31 Box 49
Midland TX 79707

KA5WFO
Clawson V Pipkin
Rt 7 Box 834
Midland TX 79701

KE5TKJ
George Johns
2213 Boyd
Midland TX 79705

KE0FE
Franklin D Henson
3406 Boyd
Midland TX 79707

N5QDQ
Jerermy J Kennedy
5101 Brazos
Midland TX 79707

N5QGL
David R Moore
5006 Brazos Ave
Midland TX 79707

KD5HAA
James T Lindenmuth
5307 Brazos Ct
Midland TX 79707

KE5ZLD
Jeff D Parker
1113 Breckenridge Dr
Midland TX 79705

KF5MQQ
Faith E Vedder
1113 Breckenridge Dr
Midland TX 79705

KF5VED
Faith E Vedder
1113 Breckenridge Dr
Midland TX 79705

KD5C
Bryant W Saxon Sr
5006 Briarpath Dr
Midland TX 79707

KF5MJR
Kurt E Kotenberg
3200 Bromley Pl Apt I301
Midland TX 79705

KD5GZZ
Greggory R Hill
4707 Brookdale
Midland TX 79703

KB5MFM
David C Thomas
4401 Brookdale Dr
Midland TX 79703

KB5MFN
David D Thomas
4401 Brookdale Dr
Midland TX 79703

WB0AOO
Brad L Cox
4616 Brookdale Dr
Midland TX 79703

KB5ZTL
Clifton M Hines
3502 Caldera
Midland TX 79707

N5XXG
Floyd S Phillips
3609 Caldera 248
Midland TX 79705

KB5ZTK
Angela K Hines
3502 Caldera Blvd
Midland TX 79707

KF5CCF
Brian M Littlejohn
3100 Caldera Blvd 1412
Midland TX 79705

KF5CCE
Joshua W Wallender
3609 Caldera Blvd 155
Midland TX 79707

N5YOC
Harold L Silverman
3609 Caldera Blvd 173
Midland TX 76707

KE5HFU
Rebecca L Gould
3100 Caldera Blvd -2211
Midland TX 79705

KF5PEM
Greg A Rule
3100 Caldera Blvd Apt 2413
Midland TX 79705

KE5MKZ
Barbara E Drissel
3229 Camarie
Midland TX 79705

KE5DYW
Sean L Kator
3314 Camarie
Midland TX 79707

KE5MKK
John C Drissel
3229 Camarie Ave
Midland TX 797056203

KE5ART
Wayne C Patterson
3313 Camarie Ave
Midland TX 797075702

KE5TKS
Antonio R Torres
1102 Canyon Dr
Midland TX 79703

WB5MDL
Aubrey L Cardwell
3308 Cardinal Ln

Midland TX 79707

W5RVV
Aubrey L Cardwell
3408 Cardinal Ln
Midland TX 79707

KE5DTT
Paul T Seegers
3708 Cardinal Ln
Midland TX 79707

KF5UY
Perry K Hurlbut
2100 Castleford 116
Midland TX 797055260

KC5ALK
Roger P Columbus
1307 Castleford Rd
Midland TX 79705

KD5OGJ
Daniel C Atkinson
1921 Centerview
Midland TX 79707

KF5BTU
Sarah E Atkinson
1921 Centerview
Midland TX 79707

KD5DRP
Richard W Wilburn
1219 Century
Midland TX 79703

W5MAF
 West Texas Skywarn
Association
2500 Challenger Dr
Midland TX 79706

KB5GCS
Joseph G Rhode
4 Chatham Ct
Midland TX 79705

WA5SVS
Norman E Williams
2609 Cimmaron
Midland TX 79705

KA5NEW

Linda S Chitwood
3802 Cimmaron
Midland TX 79707

KB5NJR
Michael R Lloyd
3229 Cimmaron Ave
Midland TX 797056210

WA5PFI
John R Wilder III
4508 CloudcroFort Ct
Midland TX 79707

WB5JLG
George P Parker
104 Club Dr
Midland TX 79701

AD5DN
Robert P Thorn Jr
204 Club Dr
Midland TX 79701

KD5HGD
Lawrence D Osborn
4104 Compton Dr
Midland TX 79707

W5UZH
James E Davis Jr
5308 Conroe Ct
Midland TX 79707

KD5VOZ
Kelin F Jones
4310 Country Club
Midland TX 79703

KD5VPA
Joshua P Jones
4310 Country Club
Midland TX 79703

WA5IOB
Edith M Hood
2008 Country Club Dr
Midland TX 797015719

N5QPF
Elmer E Howard
3209 CR 1066 S
Midland TX 79701

WB5AHS
Frank T Meyer
9905 CR 152 West
Midland TX 79703

N5SVM
Allan B Moore Mr
6208 CR 57
Midland TX 79705

KE5MBN
Charles R Stigen
6205 CR 67 East
Midland TX 79705

KF5AUL
Andrew S Fierro
5703 Cranston Pl
Midland TX 79707

WB5UTD
Patrick D Rasavage
5707 Cranston Pl
Midland TX 79707

KD5TZR
Kevin M Morris
3909 Crestgate
Midland TX 797072714

N5SOR
Mark T Lomax
4102 Crestgate
Midland TX 79707

KF5KTT
Keaton Vines
3908 Crestline
Midland TX 79707

KM5IF
Wayne A Sims
3701 Crestmont Dr
Midland TX 79707

KD5LRF
William R Lawless
4000 Crestridge
Midland TX 79707

KD5TLZ
 Permian Basin Amateur Radio
Club
4000 Crestridge

Midland TX 79707

W5PBR
Permian Basin Amateur Radio
Club
4000 Crestridge
Midland TX 79707

W5WRL
William R Lawless
4000 Crestridge
Midland TX 79707

KC5WUO
Donald R Fraley
4716 Crockett
Midland TX 79703

KE5ZLE
Christine D De Socarraz
5605 Crowley Blvd
Midland TX 79707

KB5TUL
Gabriel Medellin Jr
1701 Culver
Midland TX 79705

K5VO
William B Wise
2406 Dartmouth Dr
Midland TX 79705

KD5RZ
Calvin R Christopher
4603 Debbie Cove
Midland TX 797075239

KB5JEZ
Gary J Ruback
4331 Dengar 211
Midland TX 79707

WB5PYT
Curtis L Mcknight III
3504 Dentcrest
Midland TX 79707

KB5ZNE
William B Martin
1012 Denton
Midland TX 79703

N1AUS

Paul K Mitchell
1005 Denton St
Midland TX 797035008

KC5DTB
Scott E Sheward
1800 Devonshire
Midland TX 79705

KL2HC
Manon T Moore
5004 Diamond Dr
Midland TX 79707

KD5ONX
Midland Amateur Radio Club
3504 Douglas
Midland TX 79703

N5UFU
E Carol Reid
3504 Douglas
Midland TX 79703

W5CAF
Commemorative Air Force Arc
3504 Douglas
Midland TX 79703

W5QGG
Midland Amateur Radio Club
3504 Douglas
Midland TX 79703

N5TQU
David L Nix
3900 Douglas
Midland TX 79703

N5TQV
William R Nix
3900 Douglas
Midland TX 79703

KB5TUP
Martha N Nix
3900 Douglas Ave
Midland TX 79703

K5KUX
James M Reid
3504 Douglas St
Midland TX 79703

N5SVB
Hans E Sheline
6503 Driftwood Dr
Midland TX 79707

W5EFX
Evan M Bouten
6009 East C Rd 86
Midland TX 79706

KD5RWU
Evan M Bouten
6009 East C Rd 86 A
Midland TX 79706

W5KAS
Kedric A Sewell
5720 East County Rd 96
Midland TX 79706

KE5PAO
Jon G Baumann
6601 East CR 105
Midland TX 79706

W5JGB
Jon G Baumann
6601 East CR 105
Midland TX 79706

W5UWQ
M J Clark
1105 East CR 120
Midland TX 797064031

KE5TKI
Dusty R Land
13401 East CR 120
Midland TX 79706

KE5MKO
Rochelle Sebree
5401 East CR 120 3
Midland TX 79706

KE5MKP
Gary E Robinson
5401 East CR 120 Southeast 3
Midland TX 79706

WA0OUK
Rita R Purcell
1207 East CR 124
Midland TX 797066501

WA0OUL
James T Purcell
1207 East CR 124
Midland TX 797066501

KD5NRZ
Curtis Witt
526 East CR 136
Midland TX 79706

KF5ENH
Landon G Bell
12700 East CR 138
Midland TX 79706

WB5RJI
Charles D Anderle
5707 East CR 57
Midland TX 79705

KE5DYT
Jacinda A Moore
6208 East CR 57
Midland TX 79705

KE5JAM
Jacinda A Moore
6208 East CR 57
Midland TX 79705

KE5MKS
Bob H Mayo
5712 East CR 65
Midland TX 79705

KE5EZD
Judith L Siefker
7305 East CR 90
Midland TX 79706

N5NA
Alan C Sewell
5720 East CR 96
Midland TX 79706

K5AKS
Andrea K Sewell
5720 East CR 96
Midland TX 79706

K6FET
Larry A Jones

1900 East Golf Course Rd Apt
1603
Midland TX 79701

N5OKO
Larry G Mitchell
1900 East Golf Course Rd Apt
401
Midland TX 797012512

KD5NVV
Virginia Smith Byrd
3405 East Hwy 80
Midland TX 79706

W5XXX
Darrell J Byrd
3405 East Hwy 80
Midland TX 79706

KB5TUN
Billy D Salyers
5501 East Hwy 80 52
Midland TX 79701

KD5VFU
Norman D Swango Jr
5501 East Hwy 80 Trlr 52
Midland TX 79706

WA5CVO
William H Wright
1600 East Magnolia
Midland TX 79705

KE5MKF
Larry J Woodruff
1924 East Pecan
Midland TX 79705

KF5EJA
Dale K Rittenhouse Jr
4200 East State Hwy 158
Midland TX 79706

KE5MKH
Ronald J England
4100 East State Hwy 158 Lot 22
Midland TX 79706

KD5SSM
Wade Moeller
5011 East State Hwy 158 Unit D
Midland TX 79706

KC5KFZ
Deborah R Bentley
400 Eastwood Dr
Midland TX 79703

N5POB
William T Bentley
400 Eastwood Dr
Midland TX 79703

KD5HGE
Trey Watkins
8403 ECR 103
Midland TX 79706

KE5EZA
Taylor A Harrell
10804 ECR 107
Midland TX 79706

KD5VOV
Joe W Wallender
10804 ECR 108
Midland TX 79706

KE5MOO
Ashley D Favinger
5401 ECR 120 Sp 3
Midland TX 79706

KE5TKL
David A Hardesty
1300 ECR 130
Midland TX 79706

KE5EYY
Kedric A Sewell
5720 ECR 96
Midland TX 79706

KE5EYZ
Aubrey C Sewell
5720 ECR 96
Midland TX 79706

KE5MKJ
Christopher M Earp
3701 Edgemont Dr
Midland TX 79707

KB5RTL
Peter V Balog
2508 Elizabeth

Midland TX 79706

KB5TUJ
Kay W Balog
2508 Elizabeth Ave
Midland TX 797016844

N5OHB
Edward E Miller
3230 Elma Dr
Midland TX 797075218

KK5ZG
Joe E Coldewey
4510 Fairbanks
Midland TX 79707

WB5IKX
Homer T Fort
9 Fairfax Ct
Midland TX 79705

KE5HGC
John M Kerrigan
3804 Fairhaven Court
Midland TX 79707

KE5ARR
Joseph A Shephard
2505 Fairview Ln
Midland TX 79705

N5RGH
Joseph A Shephard
2505 Fairview Ln
Midland TX 79705

KD5OUZ
Curtis L Mcknight III
2311 Fannin
Midland TX 79705

WB5MSP
Norman S Gould
2814 Fannin
Midland TX 797056109

W5PKD
Frank M Smith
5613 Fenway
Midland TX 79707

KF5FGY
Caleb L Kircus

4210 Ferncliff Ave
Midland TX 79707

WA5IKX
Royce D Rowden
5111 FM 715 Sp 8
Midland TX 79706

AA5ID
Thomas K Coleman
4905 Foxboro Ct
Midland TX 79705

KD5QIL
Tina L Coleman
4905 Foxboro Ct
Midland TX 79705

KF5AOA
James C Dyer
2700 Franklin
Midland TX 79701

KC5KFX
Henry Anderle
3213 Frontier
Midland TX 79705

KC7LBM
Daniel G Penny II
601 George Ave 103
Midland TX 79705

KD7OKM
Sara J Penny
601 George Ave 103
Midland TX 79705

W5RQZ
Sarah E Tarter
4007 Gleneagles
Midland TX 79707

WA5NNM
Henry K Smith
2414 Goddard Ct
Midland TX 79705

N5OVH
Albert R Karch
2503 Goddard Dr
Midland TX 79705

KF5EGD

Walter W Oaks
2508 Goddard Dr
Midland TX 79705

KD5JJI
Robert L Bonnington
2820 Goddard Pl
Midland TX 79705

WA0ZHH
Charles B Seeton
3601 Godfrey Ct
Midland TX 79707

KF5PEL
Jeremy J Kennedy
4101 Godfrey St
Midland TX 79707

K5JXN
Robert H Stevens
4623 Graceland Dr
Midland TX 79703

KC5KZJ
George E Sitton
5622 Grassland Blvd
Midland TX 797075006

WD9AHU
Susan D Kochanski
5308 Green Tree Blvd
Midland TX 79707

WA5VUE
Ted E Armacost
5801 Greenridge
Midland TX 797079772

AD5N
Robert L Mims Sr
2410 Gulf
Midland TX 79701

W5MVC
Robert G Edgerton
4406 Gulf
Midland TX 79703

K5IAG
Dino R Parenti
810 Gulf Ave
Midland TX 79705

KC5GUV
Joe M Cummins
3600 Gulf Ave
Midland TX 79707

KE5DYR
Steven E Ingram
5501 Hathaway
Midland TX 79707

KD5VOW
Eddie A Ingram
5501 Hathaway Ct
Midland TX 79707

KE5WCL
Ragnvald H Olsen
5601 Heartland Ct
Midland TX 79707

KE5MKI
Sonja L Brekke
1900 Hereford Blvd
Midland TX 79707

KB5MBK
William P England
1900 Hereford Blvd
Midland TX 79707

KC0EPF
Patrick L Vesper
1904 Hereford Blvd
Midland TX 79707

KC5BHZ
Kimber Lea Mc Lennan
5507 Highland Ct
Midland TX 797075017

KE5ZLB
Shane A Perley
201 Howard
Midland TX 79703

K9ING
Robert L Stevens
2207 Hughes
Midland TX 79701

KC5WUN
Tommy R Merrill
6508 Hwy 307
Midland TX 79701

KD5ADI
Julian A Hooker
508B Hyde Park
Midland TX 79707

KB5YYS
Donnie W Barber
2415 Idlewilde Dr 7
Midland TX 79707

K0ITF
Olen G Bunting
4604 Island Dr
Midland TX 79707

W5RDD
Richard D Dunham
4701 Island Dr
Midland TX 79707

WB5ZPE
Richard D Dunham
4701 Island Dr
Midland TX 79707

KF5CCD
Philip M Robb
4807 Island Dr
Midland TX 79707

WB5ANU
Dee C Pollard
3611 Jordan
Midland TX 79707

K5RSX
Richard A Shelton
5025 Joy Dr
Midland TX 79703

KE5WZH
Richard A Shelton
5025 Joy Dr
Midland TX 79703

KD5OXO
Alan T Mccurdy
4923 Keenland Dr
Midland TX 79707

KB5RRY
Charles R Hall
2605 Keswick Cv

Midland TX 79705

KE5FE
Myrl W Robinson
2400 Keswick Rd
Midland TX 79705

N5NSJ
Edward B Curran
2402 Keswick Rd
Midland TX 79705

KE5TKF
Dan Meador
4608 Kiowa Dr
Midland TX 79703

KE5ZLG
Rae Bellamy
4304 Kniffen
Midland TX 79705

KD5CRN
Michael I Ham
1403 Lanham
Midland TX 79701

N5IDJ
David G Campbell
4422 Lanham St
Midland TX 79705

KA5HWF
John R Tidwell
4610 Laura
Midland TX 79703

KD5MQC
William R Long
5212 Lavaca Ave
Midland TX 79707

KE5TKT
Charles A Evans
5309 Lavaca Ave
Midland TX 79707

KN5M
Troy D Lesley
2505 Learmont Dr
Midland TX 79705

KE5HFS
Patrick J Repman

4509 Leddy
Midland TX 79703

KC5LRK
Ronald G Eng
4722 Leisure Dr
Midland TX 79703

WA5PFJ
John R Wilder Jr
4405 Lennox Dr
Midland TX 79707

KB5ELP
Jeremy T Moore
6006 Little John Ln
Midland TX 79707

KD5MKD
Karl R Heimke
5013 Los Alamitos
Midland TX 79705

KE5IAZ
Keith A Hunter Jr
5013 Los Alamitos
Midland TX 79705

KE5MKX
William D Seago
3307 Louisiana
Midland TX 79703

KE5ZLF
Shirley A Clifton
3110 Ma Mar
Midland TX 79705

N5MWV
Thomas I Coleman Jr
1705 Maberry
Midland TX 79705

W5MLS
Michael L Smith
300 Maraina Ave Apt A
Midland TX 79701

N5JX
James L Greene III
2409 Maxwell
Midland TX 79705

K5CFA

Donald R Mc Carty
2304 Maxwell Dr
Midland TX 79705

NV5R
Carla J Mc Carty
2304 Maxwell Dr
Midland TX 79705

N5QB
William J Mewhorter
2310 Maxwell Dr
Midland TX 79705

KE5TKC
Grier O Phillips
2602 Maxwell Dr
Midland TX 79705

W5NUB
Joel T Blankenship
2607 Maxwell Dr
Midland TX 79701

KE5MKV
Dwain E Schumacher
1402 Mcdonald
Midland TX 79703

W5EBO
Howard T Bentley
1500 McDonald
Midland TX 79703

WA5STG
Norma M Bentley
1500 McDonald
Midland TX 79703

N2JDE
Michael Leyba
1602 McDonald St
Midland TX 79703

KD5UIB
Glen W Tabor
4506 Meredith Pl
Midland TX 79707

KE5MKU
Joe Hathaway
2825 Metz Dr
Midland TX 797054900

KD5QFA
Carolyn S Parsons
3601 Mockingbird Ln
Midland TX 79707

KE5ARW
Jonathan T Lambdin
700 Mogford
Midland TX 79701

WV5E
Thomas T Lambdin
700 Mogford
Midland TX 79701

WB5RCD
Mark S Dill
704 Mogford
Midland TX 79701

WB5IWP
Mary A Stice
4306 Monty
Midland TX 79703

WB5JFE
Kurt T Shedeck
2307 Neely
Midland TX 79705

WD5EPP
Deborah K Mc Cleery
3804 Neely Ave
Midland TX 79707

NX5E
John K Peterson
2300 North A St 1904
Midland TX 797057639

KB5RGF
Kevin A Silva
5101 North A St Apt 274
Midland TX 79705

KE5FEJ
David F Ham
4207 North Cnty Rd 1243
Midland TX 79707

KD5OXN
Kevin J Laman
4313 North County Rd 1283
Midland TX 79707

KE5TJY
Harry E Washam Jr
118 North Dewberry
Midland TX 79703

WD5HOD
Tommy L White Jr
106 North Eisenhower
Midland TX 79703

KF5LRL
Chris J Young
1607 North Garfield
Midland TX 79701

K5YR
Robert B Mc Cleery
201 North Glenwood
Midland TX 79701

KT5G
Bill N Anderson
311 North Godfrey St
Midland TX 79703

KF3DD
Delbert D Dick
4400 North Holiday Hill Rd Apt
611
Midland TX 79707

KF5IGC
Matthew A Vann
1610 North J St
Midland TX 79701

N5MAV
Matthew A Vann
1610 North J St
Midland TX 79701

KB5ZVA
Pete J Arroyo
5266 North Loop 250 West
Midland TX 79706

K5PSA
 Public Safety Amateur Radio
Association Of The Permian
Basin
601 North Loraine
Midland TX 79701

KE5DXR
 Public Safety Amateur Radio
Association Of The Permian
Basin
601 North Loraine
Midland TX 79701

KE5EZE
John C Beane
4712 North Midkiff
Midland TX 79705

KE4ZJH
Joseph F Svacek III
3600 North Midland Dr 1F
Midland TX 79707

KC5IPQ
James C Walter
4415 Northcrest 2324
Midland TX 79707

N5EUM
Ralph C Huggins
2607 Northrup
Midland TX 79705

KQ4MW
Dallas E Mays
5903 Nottingham Ln
Midland TX 79707

KB5VRN
Christy M Lannom
6209 Ojibwa
Midland TX 79705

KE5VXL
Christy M Lannom
6209 Ojibwa
Midland TX 79705

N5MXE
Clint A Lannom
6209 Ojibwa
Midland TX 79705

KD5RWW
Richard N Alden
6202 Ojibwa St
Midland TX 79705

W5LKL
Buck M Williford

705 Osage St
Midland TX 79705

KF5FGX
Ronald E Kircus
P O Box 80862
Midland TX 79708

W5STC
Clyde R Schwisow
806 Palomino
Midland TX 79701

KZ5H
Clyde R Schwisow
806 Palomino
Midland TX 797051811

KB5MUD
Paul D Lloyd
4502 Parkdale
Midland TX 79703

WA5SMQ
David R Lloyd
4502 Parkdale
Midland TX 79703

KD5MHL
Heather M Hearn
4401 Pasadena
Midland TX 79703

KD5LRD
Jerry E Hearn
4401 Pasadena Dr
Midland TX 79703

KE5DYS
Hoy L Bryson Jr
4507 Pasadena Dr
Midland TX 79703

W5KBW
John H Eudy
3800 Permian Ct
Midland TX 79703

N5TLI
Russell E Hill
5101 Pleasant Ct
Midland TX 79703

KC5JHC

Raymond R Fagen
5008 Polo Pky
Midland TX 79705

K5RS
Stephen R Hopkins
3511 Princeton
Midland TX 79703

KE5HGI
James M Humphreys
4504 Princeton
Midland TX 797034710

KD5VOY
Paul A Jurek
3302 Providence Dr
Midland TX 79707

K5CGW
Clinton H Adams
2512 Quail Point
Midland TX 79705

KD5OXP
Michael J Carr
5128 Reeves Cr
Midland TX 79703

KE5ARS
James E Deberry Jr
2310 Regal Pl
Midland TX 797076252

KE5MKW
Roderick J Hennessy
4720 Ric Dr
Midland TX 797035316

KE5ZLA
Gilberto M Aguirre
5103 Ric Dr
Midland TX 79703

KF5ILO
Kirit N Patel
5709 Ridgemont Pl
Midland TX 79707

KB5YYR
Trichelle F Barber
4515 Robin Ln
Midland TX 79707

KB5STI
Wilton E Youngblood
4515 Robin Ln
Midland TX 79707

KB5STJ
Gloria F Youngblood
4515 Robin Ln
Midland TX 79707

N5KNB
James E Radtke
309 Rocky Ln
Midland TX 79703

KE5HFT
David Flores
3900 Roosevelt
Midland TX 79705

KB5MHP
Rick L Watt
4006 Roosevelt
Midland TX 797036127

W5SUP
William J Shields
4010 Roosevelt
Midland TX 79703

WA5QZX
Howard A Palmer Jr
3808 Roosevelt Dr
Midland TX 79703

WB5TCW
David S Turner
18 Saddle Club Dr
Midland TX 797051834

KD5MWI
Kristi J Mcknight
5714 San Saba
Midland TX 79707

KE5NFU
Kendall L Robinson
3203 SCR 1066
Midland TX 79706

KE5NFV
Justin A Robinson
3203 SCR 1066
Midland TX 79706

KD5HJP
Johnnie K Eubanks
3200 SCR 1068
Midland TX 79706

KE5DYU
Dudley E Speed
2909 SCR 1083
Midland TX 79706

KF5BCS
Allen L Graham
1917 SCR 1085
Midland TX 79710

KE5ATX
Gary L Goodman
3805 SCR 1184
Midland TX 79706

KC5ETV
Les M Bradshaw
3516 SCR 1198
Midland TX 79706

K5PDL
Paul D Laverty
1500 Seaboard
Midland TX 79705

KD5TEB
Paul D Laverty
1500 Seaboard
Midland TX 79705

KE5HGF
Troy E Hively
1503 Seaboard Ave
Midland TX 79705

N5UAI
Roy E Marshall
3501 Sentinel
Midland TX 79703

KB5RTW
Daniel F Secker
2904 Sentinel Dr
Midland TX 79701

KE5QQX
Bryce C Gaston
3103 Shell

Midland TX 79705

KF5KGM
Paul D Talley
1003 Shell Ave
Midland TX 79705

W5RCB
Richard W Titchen
3203 Sinclair Ave
Midland TX 797058239

KI5LB
David R Rowe
1402 Sioux Ct
Midland TX 79705

W5MU
Wesley E Pittman
907 Sorrel Ln West
Midland TX 79705

KD5WKX
James F Kennedy IV
300 South Baird
Midland TX 79701

KD5QCN
James M Bowen
101 South Bentwood
Midland TX 79703

KD5SDW
Clayton M Smith
502 South Bentwood
Midland TX 79703

N5UNH
Clayton M Smith
502 South Bentwood
Midland TX 79703

N5UNH
Mark D Smith
502 South Bentwood
Midland TX 79703

WB5EZR
James R Porterfield Sr
1700 South Camp
Midland TX 79701

KB5W
Lee E Ligon

6301 South CR 1065
Midland TX 79706

N5LTT
Lee E Ligon
6301 South CR 1065
Midland TX 79706

KB5NAD
Sandra M Howard
3209 South CR 1066
Midland TX 79701

KB5PJR
Rachel L Howard
3209 South CR 1066
Midland TX 79701

KB5PKN
Elmer E Howard Jr
3209 South CR 1066
Midland TX 79701

KB5RGU
William D Howard
3209 South CR 1066
Midland TX 79701

N5XXP
Hoyt D Handley
1202 South CR 1082
Midland TX 79706

KC5OI
Allan T Schmidt
2201 South CR 1105
Midland TX 79706

KF5HYP
David A Bell
2423 South CR 1120
Midland TX 79706

K5MTX
Douglas G Harwood
6100 South CR 1169
Midland TX 797067700

KF5BCT
Everett L Foreman III
6101 South CR 1169
Midland TX 79706

W5GBQ

James R Giles
4908 South CR 1178
Midland TX 78706

WA5ZFH
James T Caldwell
3705 South CR 1184
Midland TX 79706

K5ZVW
William R Harral
3805 South CR 1187
Midland TX 79706

KA5EEL
Billy L Smith
2907 South CR 1210
Midland TX 79706

K5JOG
Floyd K Williams
9700 South CR 1218
Midland TX 797067812

AE5J
Banks Campbell Jr
2703 South CR 1223
Midland TX 79706

K5YUM
Brenda S Campbell Jr
2703 South CR 1223
Midland TX 79706

WB5WFZ
Brenda S Campbell Jr
2703 South CR 1223
Midland TX 79706

KB5RTN
William C Winslett
2917 South CR 1223 12
Midland TX 79703

KD5HGB
Johnny L Bragg
6402 South CR 1288
Midland TX 79706

KD5HRN
Kelan M Roy
306 South Eisenhower
Midland TX 79703

WA4UHV
Charles D Samples
1204 South Fort Worth
Midland TX 79701

N5FYM
John L Evans
4705 South Hwy 349
Midland TX 79706

KD5VOX
Robert M Lovelady
1003 South Midkiff Ste 2101
Midland TX 79701

N5JHX
Jerry E Hearn
4508 Spence Dr
Midland TX 79707

WB5CDD
Dewey D Baucum
707 Spraberry Dr
Midland TX 79703

W5VNS
Stanley J Krawiec
4210 St Andrews
Midland TX 79707

KE5EZB
Covan L Banner
801 Stanolind
Midland TX 79705

KA5LLS
Gregory G Banner
801 Stanolind
Midland TX 797057538

N5ATO
Gregory G Banner
801 Stanolind
Midland TX 797057538

KD5QII
David B Reyes
1008 Stanolind
Midland TX 79705

KE5EZC
Melvin D Little
3517 Stanolind
Midland TX 79707

KD5DRO
Janet L Mc Daniel
4902 Stoneleigh
Midland TX 79705

KE5PL
Boyd J Mc Daniel
4902 Stoneleigh Dr
Midland TX 79705

KE5GDY
Robert E Doerr Jr
5008 Stoneleigh Dr
Midland TX 79705

W5LXS
Roger C Rose
1409 Storey Ave
Midland TX 797016006

KD5SYJ
Larry M Kirby
4711 Storey Ave
Midland TX 79703

WA5UTR
Odie H Bridgewater Jr
4821 Storey Ave
Midland TX 797035324

N5YYS
John R Ragan
5105 Storey Ave
Midland TX 79703

W5EOC
 Midland County Amateur
Radio Emergency Service
4325 B Storey Ave
Midland TX 79703

W5ZOX
Dwayne T Fox
4325 B Storey Ave
Midland TX 79703

WD5HZJ
Roy H Chamberlain
706 Storey St
Midland TX 79701

KA5IDJ
Mark E Bozzell

3 Stutz Ct
Midland TX 79705

W5CCE
Charles A Evans
3210 Stutz Dr
Midland TX 79705

KA5BJF
Joe B Thomas
2306 Stutz Pl
Midland TX 79701

KC5DSZ
Stephen M Johnson
3805 Suncrest
Midland TX 79707

KF5FUD
James E Smith
5102 Sunnyside Dr
Midland TX 79703

N5LUA
Saundra E Hill
3305 Tanner
Midland TX 79703

KA5OCY
Robert E Doyle
3604 Tanner Dr
Midland TX 79703

KE5SYA
Ronald W Bonkrude
1002 Tarleton St
Midland TX 79703

KE5TKD
J Mike Peek
3122 Tealwood Pl
Midland TX 79705

KE5MLP
Lonnie C Yee
3207 Tealwood Pl
Midland TX 79705

KC5PHM
C Dian Dedon
1303 Tejas
Midland TX 79705

N5WT

Franklin L Dedon
1303 Tejas
Midland TX 79705

K5PQK
John L Ponder
2309 Terrace
Midland TX 79705

KD5VFT
Jimmy V Andrews
2411 Terrace
Midland TX 79705

KC5KZK
Gregory L Wootan
4506 Thomason Dr
Midland TX 797036947

K5NAA
Nancy A Alkire
4410A Thomason Dr
Midland TX 79703

KB5VGJ
Robert M Wornell
3902 Thomason Dr
Midland TX 79703

K5TOM
Tommy M Martin
4300 Thornberry
Midland TX 79707

KB5RGV
Matthew L Buck
3609 Travis
Midland TX 79703

KD5ILO
David S Googins III
3501 Trinity Meadows Dr
Midland TX 797074532

KD5AAU
Spencer S Wood
4111 Tumbleweed Trl
Midland TX 79707

W5AJ
Robert A Wood
4111 Tumbleweed Trl
Midland TX 79707

WJ5DX
West Texas Dx Club
4111 Tumblewood Trl
Midland TX 79707

W5LNX
Southwest Lynx System Arc
1401 Ventura
Midland TX 79705

WB5G
Sterling J Talley
1401 Ventura
Midland TX 79705

K5BZ
Midland Ve Team Arc
1401 Ventura
Midland TX 797056540

N5UWQ
Mary L Talley
1401 Ventura
Midland TX 797056540

KD5AAQ
Theldon K Odom
5007 Wcr 116 83
Midland TX 79706

KD5JTG
Jeremiah A Cain
1008 Wcr 150
Midland TX 79706

KD5JHU
Midland County Sheriff'S
Office
3611 Wedgewood
Midland TX 79707

W5KGX
Robert O Lowery
607 West Broadway
Midland TX 79701

K7EZT
Thomas M Gifford
10600 West Co Rd 143 12
Midland TX 797063016

KD5LRE
Bradley S Kuhn
11108 West Co Rd 150

Midland TX 79706

N5NOH
Wesley G Clements
2911 West CR 110
Midland TX 79703

N5GTO
Thomas E Kuhn Jr
11108 West CR 150
Midland TX 797063035

W5WPH
Fred M Michna
3319 West CR 185
Midland TX 79706

AE5BM
John C Mezera
3322 West CR 185
Midland TX 79706

KA5DOU
John C Mezera
3322 West CR 185
Midland TX 79706

K5VLN
Calvin W White
11421 West CR 30
Midland TX 797078924

KC5FFG
James R Buice
12010 West CR 52
Midland TX 79707

WA5ZAP
Robert M Martin
10319 West CR 56
Midland TX 79707

KE5ARV
Eric M Platt
11507 West CR 56
Midland TX 79707

KD5JJH
Roger B Fox
4722 West Cuthbert Ave
Midland TX 79703

KC5LWH
Gary L Gibson

4331 West Dengar 201
Midland TX 79707

W5UA
Joe T Milam
4732 West Dengar Ave
Midland TX 797075203

AG5A
Ralph B Miller
3303 West Douglas Ave
Midland TX 79703

N5CLR
James C Washburn
1606 West Golf Course Rd
Midland TX 79701

KE5OB
Edwin R Mickle
3200 West Golf Course Rd
Midland TX 79705

KB5RGR
Angel R Karch
305 West Hamby Ave
Midland TX 79701

KD5AAP
Edward L St John
4822 West Illinois
Midland TX 79703

KB5QBU
Donald J Kelly
3000 West Illinois 1
Midland TX 79701

K5TYY
Ray P Moudy
3000 West Illinois 3
Midland TX 79701

WA5ETE
Jerald H Bartley
1705 West Illinois Ave
Midland TX 79701

KC6ZEI
Read B Johnston
3114 West Illinois Ave
Midland TX 79701

KC5MAI

Michael E Partusch
4000 West Illinois Ave 248
Midland TX 79703

KA5IPM
Landon L Soles
3115 West Kansas
Midland TX 79701

N5OGQ
Bruce H White
2405 West Kansas Ave
Midland TX 79701

KE5QLT
Stephen B Gibson
3600 West Loop 250 North
Midland TX 79707

KE4MKZ
Robert P Thorn Jr
2600 West Loop 250 North 403
Midland TX 79505

W5HJE
Leslie E Long
3600 West Loop 250 North Apt
1113
Midland TX 79707

KE5VEF
Michelle L Schuldt
3600 West Loop 250 North Apt
2016
Midland TX 79707

KM5OK
C A Ross Jr
3507 West Louisiana
Midland TX 797036545

K5KTY
Alvin N Moore
3518 West Louisiana
Midland TX 79703

N5XXD
Mark Cranford
1404 West Louisiana Ave
Midland TX 79701

N5ZMP
Sara G P Cranford
1404 West Louisiana Ave

Midland TX 797016048

KB5TUK
Felicia K Nettles
2003 West Michigan
Midland TX 79701

N5UNI
James E Nettles
2003 West Michigan
Midland TX 797015925

N5HXW
Jerome H Codington
3100 West Michigan
Midland TX 79701

KF5LQO
Juanita A Carrasco
712 West Michigan 15
Midland TX 79701

KC5VCD
Tina M Briley
3506 West Michigan Ave
Midland TX 797035614

KK5RJ
Bryan N Briley
3506 West Michigan Ave
Midland TX 797035614

W5KPE
C M Elmore Jr
3712 West Michigan Ave
Midland TX 797035523

KD5UFE
Chris S Berard
1408 West Missouri
Midland TX 79701

WA5IPY
James W Kerr
3522 West Ohio
Midland TX 79703

KB5RGE
John H Carson
1502 West Pine
Midland TX 79705

KB5RTX
Noressa L Carson

1502 West Pine
Midland TX 79705

N5WCT
Milton G Hathaway
501 West Scharbauer 38
Midland TX 79705

KC5LFW
Jennifer M Reck
3313 West Shandon
Midland TX 79707

KF5EJB
Ben L Turpen
2828 West Shandon Ave
Midland TX 79705

W5AYK
Louis S Torrans Jr
3225 West Shandon Ave
Midland TX 797056249

W5VSN
Maxine E Torrans
3225 West Shandon Ave
Midland TX 797056249

KC5NXK
Jose L Gardea
3306 West Storey
Midland TX 79703

KE5DYV
John C Mitchick
2503 West Storey Ave
Midland TX 797015652

KB5ACV
Shellie D Laird
2501 West Story
Midland TX 79701

KB5KQE
Karen N Eggleston
1605 West Tennessee
Midland TX 79701

KI5AS
David M Eggleston
1605 West Tennessee
Midland TX 79701

N5OOR

Eric D Eggleston
1605 West Tennessee
Midland TX 79701

KF5MPI
Karl R Boland
3327 West Wadley Ave 3-118
Midland TX 79707

W3QKC
William A Palmisano
2100 West Wadley-Apt 14
Midland TX 797056434

NC5F
Jay B Gibson
2438 Whitmire Blvd Apt 12F
Midland TX 79705

KF5OLS
Daniel R Russell
2433 Whitmire Blvd Apt 69
Midland TX 79705

KF5JCM
Ryan T Speer
2105 Whitney
Midland TX 79705

KB5YBN
Richard E Biggerstaff Jr
2601 Whittle Way
Midland TX 79707

WA5UFO
Markus D Thomerson
3401 Whittle Way
Midland TX 79707

KE5MKR
Justin D Bunch
320 Willowood
Midland TX 79703

KE5TKH
Dylan D Morgan
329 Willowood
Midland TX 79703

KE5MKT
James D Morgan
329 Willowood
Midland TX 797036318

KE5TKG
Tyler F Morgan
329 Willowood Dr
Midland TX 79703

K5ZIS
Omer A Wickman
1601 Winfield Rd
Midland TX 79705

W5BPA
James R Williams
408 Woodcrest Dr
Midland TX 797035335

N5VHS
Rory L Lacy
2205 Wydewood Dr
Midland TX 79707

K5GWP
Gary Painter
Midland TX 79701

KE5EZF
Gary Painter
Midland TX 79701

K5MSO
Midland County Sheriff'S
Office
Midland TX 79702

KA5ZKA
David N Grimes
Midland TX 79702

KB5DEM
David J Carlson
Midland TX 79702

KE5SYG
Wyndee Kalisek
Midland TX 79702

KE5SYM
Devin S Johnson
Midland TX 79702

KE5TKA
Horace M Slate II
Midland TX 79702

KE5VKR

Omar Rosas Jr
Midland TX 79702

KF4IWG
Lon S Platt
Midland TX 79702

N5NBR
Roger A Hyatt
Midland TX 79702

WA2LLX
John C Lambert Jr
Midland TX 79702

KC5ETY
Beth A Broughton
Midland TX 79704

KD5C
Midland Amateur Radio Club
Midland TX 79704

KE5WRS
Midland Amateur Radio Club
Midland TX 79704

N5HXV
Janie R Martin
Midland TX 79704

KD5ZQN
Randy C Mcmullen
Midland TX 79708

KE5TKE
Susanne P Mcvay
Midland TX 79708

KE5VFP
Thomas B Kingon
Midland TX 79708

KF5ODE
Cameron D Pryor
Midland TX 79708

K5SHL
Billy R Jones
Midland TX 79710

KE5TGW
Aaron R Sides
Midland TX 79710

KF5HHD
Deborah S Magness
Midland TX 79710

KG5BN
Tommy F Altman
Midland TX 79710

KD5MHM
Scott D Johnson
Midland TX 797020076

KD5VOU
Dwayne E Frantz
Midland TX 797020575

N5MGH
Raymond H Randall
Midland TX 797026162

KB5CWJ
Ralph H Lang Jr
Midland TX 797027766

KE5MON
Mark A Hannifin
Midland TX 797028182

N5VCH
Michael S Baker Mr
Midland TX 797045932

KE5HFP
Christian Amateur Radio Club
Midland TX 797110491

KD5DRH
Perry L Martin
Midland TX 797110682

KB5JIO
Tonya R Altman
Midland TX 79702

KB5JIP
Jerry W Altman
Midland TX 79702

N5RZ
Ralph E Bowen
Midland TX 79702

N5ZRK

Chad A Hyatt
Midland TX 79702

WB5AAR
Alligator Amateur Radio Club
Midland TX 79702

KC5DAD
Tommy M Martin Jr
Midland TX 79704

N5PRX
Mark E Hilton
Midland TX 79704

KA5VYR
James L Gregory
Midland TX 79708

KB5SXM
Terry K Repman
Midland TX 79708

W5GFO
Timothy V Kreitz
Midland TX 79710

FCC Amateur Radio Licenses
in Monahans

W5AWT
Melvin E Boatman
Box 1895
Monahans TX 79756

KB5TUI
Arnold B Thurmond
806 East 3rd
Monahans TX 79756

K5QOE
Robert R Spinks Sr
1400 Franklin
Monahans TX 79756

KC5PRJ
Donna M Crisp-Mapes
1105 Kenneth Ave
Monahans TX 79756

KC5EEV
Gerry E Petree
1202 Leon St
Monahans TX 79756

KD5KEZ
Gary C Burch
1507 South Allen
Monahans TX 79756

W5FQH
Russell B Bowman
405 South Eric St
Monahans TX 79756

KE5SXT
Steven D Morrison
3801 South Faye
Monahans TX 79756

WD5CBY
Clarice D Mills
1109 South Gary St
Monahans TX 79756

KK5PX
Daniel R Pipkin
4010 South Helen
Monahans TX 79756

KA5VWD
Patsy L Sligh
1602 South Ike St
Monahans TX 79756

W5RJH
Alvin P Sligh
1602 South Ike St
Monahans TX 79756

W5GDP
Glenn D Brice
904 South James
Monahans TX 79756

KE5CJD
Jeffrey D Benbow
1203 South Kenneth
Monahans TX 79756

KB5THQ
Jack T Ledingham
1201 South Leon
Monahans TX 79756

KE5CBO
Bryan T Mcdaniel
1201 South Murray

Monahans TX 79756

KD5HTQ
Jon P Calder
203 West 14th
Monahans TX 79756

WA5BTE
Bill D Stribling
2109 West 4th
Monahans TX 79756

K5FTF
Robert M Roeber
Monahans TX 79756

KD5FTF
Robert M Roeber
Monahans TX 79756

KC5OJU
Alan W Woods Sr
Monahans TX 79756

KB5EDZ
John R Middleton
Monahans TX 79756

N5QIE
Tom W Murray
Monahans TX 79756

**FCC Amateur Radio Licenses
in Odessa**

KB5MWR
Ray D Walker
2115 Adams
Odessa TX 79761

WB5RCX
William F Hause
1909 Alturas
Odessa TX 79763

KC5KZO
Brandon E Rives
6552 Amber
Odessa TX 79762

KB5WLG
Rocky G Cavanaugh
3626 Archuleta
Odessa TX 79763

KE5DYY
Steven R Ellsworth
2741 Bainbridge
Odessa TX 79762

KE5YIA
Michael J Ellsworth
2741 Bainbridge Dr
Odessa TX 74762

KE5VFO
Matthew S Ellsworth
2741 Bainbridge Dr
Odessa TX 79762

KF5FHA
Louise N Ellsworth
2741 Bainbridge Dr
Odessa TX 79762

N5LUG
Robert M Kiser
9106 Bedford
Odessa TX 79764

K5DKW
Farl R Gibson
9000 Bedford Dr
Odessa TX 79764

WA5KMH
Jerry S Dillard
2976 Beechwood St
Odessa TX 79761

KE5IBA
Mark A Malone
3124 Blossom Ln
Odessa TX 79762

N5SVE
Samuel W Howell
3214 Blossom Ln
Odessa TX 79762

K5YBY
Larry M Namken
2514 Bonham Ave
Odessa TX 79762

N5QGX
Gary R Parks
3004 Bonham Ave

Odessa TX 79762

N5GJF
Wesley J Thomason
Rt 7 Box 1674
Odessa TX 79763

KB5MQD
Paul D Carr
Rt 11 Box 2470A
Odessa TX 79763

KB5MJT
David B Stonestreet
Rt 1 Box 309
Odessa TX 79765

KB5LFA
Jim F Brayton
Rt 1 Box 309D
Odessa TX 79765

N5AJP
Carl H Goetz Jr
Box 3182
Odessa TX 79760

N5PSR
David S Mc Caffity
Rt 11 Box 9979
Odessa TX 79763

KG5BF
Alwyn L Chitwood Sr
1475 Brittany Ln 1
Odessa TX 79760

WB5NTZ
Frank R Harris
2408 Cambridge St
Odessa TX 79761

KC5ELQ
Charles A Hildebrand
4243 Candy Ln
Odessa TX 79762

N5ETX
John T Lumpkin
6525 Carter
Odessa TX 79764

N5HDH
Lou M Lumpkin

6525 Carter
Odessa TX 79764

KD5HGC
Barbara A Graff
200 Casa Grande
Odessa TX 79763

W5JWA
Billy J Hill
1513 Castle Rd
Odessa TX 79762

KB0YLB
David A Brinnen
2921 Chisum Ave
Odessa TX 79762

KB5VWD
Ken Bridges
6311 Christopher Ln
Odessa TX 797625457

KC5ELP
Victoria S Detiveaux
621 Claymoor Dr
Odessa TX 79764

WA5VYK
Sherrell J Detiveaux
621 Claymoor Dr
Odessa TX 79764

WT5ARC
West Texas Amateur Radio
Club Inc
621 Claymoor Dr
Odessa TX 79764

KA5L
Eddie R Owen Jr
4913 Clover Dr
Odessa TX 79762

KA5NCH
Jason K Owen
4913 Clover Dr
Odessa TX 79762

WD5CHI
Margaret L Owen
4913 Clover Dr
Odessa TX 79762

WA5HFU
Lloyd E Sanders Jr
1836 Cody Pl
Odessa TX 79762

N5DR
Don R Roberson
114 Conet Dr
Odessa TX 79763

N6ABM
Randolph C Miller
5008 Conley Av
Odessa TX 79762

KB5RGD
Gerald W Beazley
4408 Conley Ave
Odessa TX 79762

W5GWB
Gerald W Beazley
4408 Conley Ave
Odessa TX 79762

KB5LZS
Michael D Smith
1120 Copus
Odessa TX 79763

KB5LZT
Donald L Smith
1120 Copus
Odessa TX 79763

KB5IPE
Jeanne L Hoke
1312 Copus
Odessa TX 79763

KB5ISV
Michael V Hoke Jr
1312 Copus
Odessa TX 79763

K5NLW
Norman L Witcher
2332 Country Club Dr
Odessa TX 797625119

KE5HAY
Norman L Witcher
2332 Country Club Dr
Odessa TX 797625119

KF5LZ
Ray E Hudson
14009 CR 123W
Odessa TX 79765

NJ5C
Thomas F O Keefe
4224 Dakota St
Odessa TX 79762

KC5KZQ
Patrick N Beasley
6517 Danbar
Odessa TX 79762

KB5UAI
Scott M Dinger
2718 Deering
Odessa TX 79762

AB5MB
John A Dinger
2718 Deering Dr
Odessa TX 79762

K5KWX
David A Bone
4320 Delwood
Odessa TX 79762

K5XXN
David A Bone
4320 Delwood
Odessa TX 79762

KB5RRS
David A Bone
4320 Delwood
Odessa TX 79762

KC5NDQ
Alex D Laabs
5705 Dennard
Odessa TX 79764

KF5NI
John P Clement Jr
1303 Doran Dr
Odessa TX 79761

KE5NGP
Larry W Keene
522 Douglas Dr

Odessa TX 79762

N5SXK
Ronald L Weeden
8718 Dublin
Odessa TX 79765

K5EG
Michel R Glenn
3104 Dumont
Odessa TX 79762

AB5P
Edward J Conrad III
1712 East 10th St
Odessa TX 79761

KD5WKR
Larry L Brown
810 East 11th St
Odessa TX 79761

K5MDM
Jackson M Neece
2543 East 11th St
Odessa TX 79761

KD5TXE
Frank C Alvarado
1516 East 13th
Odessa TX 79761

N5RKN
Robert E Jordan
1521 East 13th
Odessa TX 79761

KC5WNR
Jackie L Jordan
1521 East 13th St
Odessa TX 79761

N5XXF
Gary F Peek
1906 East 13th St
Odessa TX 79761

KE5AAR
Adam F Trexler
2313 East 16th St
Odessa TX 79761

KA5REL
Jesse W Moore

906 East 18th St
Odessa TX 797611308

KB5ELO
Janice K Moore
906 East 18th St
Odessa TX 797611308

KE5ZKZ
Charles W Duke
2603 East 21st St
Odessa TX 79761

W5RCN
William R Bowden Sr
2807 East 21st St
Odessa TX 79761

KB5VWF
Frank C Alvarado
1200 East 36th
Odessa TX 79762

KB5LZR
Evelyn E Kelley
800 East 36th St
Odessa TX 79762

WA5IBE
Duward H Potts
906 East 36th St
Odessa TX 79762

N5GYF
Lawrence M Brown
415 East 43
Odessa TX 79762

AC5YR
William D Callahan
1214 East 43
Odessa TX 79762

KM5MO
William D Callahan
1214 East 43
Odessa TX 79762

N5DYA
Donald G Glenn
401 East 43
Odessa TX 79762

KE5CUF

James D Callahan
1214 East 43rd St
Odessa TX 79762

W5CBS
Glover B Brock
1126 East 44th St
Odessa TX 79762

W5CDM
Gareth M Pollard
1220 East 51st St
Odessa TX 79762

WB5RGB
Donny C Goforth
1625 East 52nd
Odessa TX 79762

KE5YHY
Dion M Delao
4136 East 52nd Apt 1606
Odessa TX 79762

N5JDC
Jonathan D Carpenter
1404 East 53rd St
Odessa TX 79762

N5ZWF
Jonathan D Carpenter
1404 East 53rd St
Odessa TX 79762

KB5WKC
Amber D Lummus
613 East 55th
Odessa TX 79762

WB5TSR
 Buffalo Trail Scout Ranch
Amat Rad Club
411 East 57th
Odessa TX 79762

WB7AMP
Rayford L Stull
306 East 57th St
Odessa TX 79762

KD5CCY
 West Texas & New Mexico
Repeater Group
409 East 57th St

Odessa TX 79762

KC5NPA
Rebecca J Norris
212 East 89th St
Odessa TX 79765

N5XXO
Rodney M Norris
212 East 89th St
Odessa TX 79765

N5YQC
Ronald E Strawser
221 East 89th St
Odessa TX 79765

KI6JLQ
Marife Orani
2735 East 8th St 122
Odessa TX 79761

WA5EHD
Morris P Barker
4010 East Everglade
Odessa TX 79762

KE5NPU
Barbara C Eddy
6401 East Ridge Rd Apt 507
Odessa TX 79762

KB5MEN
Jason W Moore
906 East St 18th
Odessa TX 79761

KF5FGZ
Dusty L Piper
2822 East University Blvd
Odessa TX 79762

KC5DGA
James R Kull
3102 Eastover Dr
Odessa TX 79762

KD5VUE
John T Bermea
6500 Eastridge Apt 3
Odessa TX 79762

KB5RRX
George I Barnes

6501 Eastridge Rd L11
Odessa TX 79762

KE5ATU
William D Callahan II
6515 Ector Ave
Odessa TX 79762

KE5OXR
Thomas E Tefertiller
3913 Elderica Ct
Odessa TX 79765

KE5CH
Gaylan C Rainey
15 Emerald Forest Dr
Odessa TX 797628421

N5KTW
Robert N Dunn
4358 Esmond
Odessa TX 76762

KB5USH
Anthony J Hamilton
4315 Esmond Dr 805
Odessa TX 79761

N5WIB
Barbara A Speidel
4315 Esmond Dr 907
Odessa TX 79762

KA5GNX
Jim B Craig
1509 Falcon
Odessa TX 79762

WA6PDK
Jay W Robinson
4520 Fountain Ct
Odessa TX 79761

KE5CIM
Geoffrey J Schwende
228 Gallant Fox Dr
Odessa TX 79763

W5JJS
Geoffrey J Schwende
228 Gallant Fox Dr
Odessa TX 79763

KB5EOF

Michael C Walker
4613 Garden Ln
Odessa TX 79762

KD5ONJ
Richard E Rausch
1104 Garnet Ave
Odessa TX 79761

N5MI
Mark D Ingram
2306 Glenwood
Odessa TX 79761

W5JLC
Jack L Cunningham
2109 Grayson Ave
Odessa TX 797611849

KD5IRB
Joe A Villarreal
2127 Hanley St
Odessa TX 79762

KE5ZKY
Joshua H Bobbett
8810 Holiday Dr
Odessa TX 79765

KD5FE
Jack L English
1810 Hollywood Dr
Odessa TX 79763

KC5ELO
Jacob L Beyerlein
10 Hummingbird Pl
Odessa TX 79761

N5LNN
Stan A Mc Vey Sr
1617 Idlewood Ln
Odessa TX 79761

KE5ZKX
Don E Hallmark
2224 Independence Dr
Odessa TX 79762

KB5IGW
Kevin B Jones
6162 Ivy Ln
Odessa TX 79762

W5QPA
Ople A Buttrell
2509 Kay
Odessa TX 79761

W5EBS
Mark H Moad
6600 Kermit Ave
Odessa TX 79762

KE5DIX
David F Wardlaw
50 Knoll Cir
Odessa TX 79762

KC5NOY
Gilbert H Galindo
1400 La Casa Dr
Odessa TX 79763

KD5IRL
Keith D Wilson
20 La Premesa Cir
Odessa TX 79765

KC6VAT
Roger M Gilden
58 Lafayette Pl
Odessa TX 79762

KA5AJW
Albert D Fox Mr
6205 Linwood Dr
Odessa TX 79762

N5JN
James H Nash
1825 Lyndale
Odessa TX 79762

WB5OJJ
Alfred M Harris
2633 Madera
Odessa TX 79763

KF5LRB
David C Golden
2125 Magill St
Odessa TX 79764

NI5T
Tresia K Thomason
2301 Marvin Ave
Odessa TX 797636302

KC5IPR
Joseph P Szaloy
4401 McKnight
Odessa TX 79762

KB5THT
Rodney B Roberts
4609 McKnight
Odessa TX 79762

N5LQF
Rodney B Roberts
4609 McKnight
Odessa TX 79762

KA5TNP
Ben L Turpen
6315 Montana
Odessa TX 79762

KF7HR
Richard J Jones
6302 Montana Ave
Odessa TX 79762

K5HCT
August N Schott
200 Monticello
Odessa TX 79763

N5GMA
James L Null
1400 North Alleghaney
Odessa TX 79761

KJ5RU
Stuart B Gaddy
1423 North Alleghaney
Odessa TX 79761

W5KPB
Trevelyn F Sparks
910 North Alleghaney Ave
Odessa TX 797613909

W5LID
Homer E Sparks
910 North Alleghany
Odessa TX 79761

KD5VPB
Ernest G Gardner
1509 North Ave J

Odessa TX 79763

KB5YOF
Carl E Bryson
1016 North Golder
Odessa TX 79761

KC5BUU
Joshua J Brindle
1111 North Golder
Odessa TX 79761

KC5ALM
Chriss S Harris
2123 North Hancock
Odessa TX 79761

N5XXM
Kenneth T Harris
2123 North Hancock
Odessa TX 79761

N5LEV
Otis E Brasfield Jr
3103 North Hancock Ave
Odessa TX 797627534

W0ICJ
Harland D Johnson Jr
5757 North Long Ave
Odessa TX 79764

KB5QQM
William W Mc Afee Jr
3101 North Moss Ave 10
Odessa TX 79763

N5HLL
William P Hopkins
1402 North Muskingum
Odessa TX 797612638

KC5ETX
Robert L Wylie Jr
423 North Rita Ave
Odessa TX 79763

KF5OOV
Caleb A Orr
2111 North Sam Houston
Odessa TX 79761

KD5PZX
Gary W Poindexter Mr

2718.5 North Tom Green
Odessa TX 79762

KD5HBB
James E Daniels
3100 North Tom Green
Odessa TX 79762

WA9JLQ
Bruce C Mc Intyre
151 North Tripp Ave
Odessa TX 79763

W5ABM
Alton B Morgan
2605 North Vega Ave
Odessa TX 79763

WB5NTI
Alton B Morgan
2605 North Vega Ave
Odessa TX 79763

KE5MKN
Dan D Wagoner
1610 North Washington
Odessa TX 79761

KB5ELM
Jane C Debenport
1703 North Washington
Odessa TX 79761

KF5LQX
Leon D Humphries
4801 Oakwood Dr 602
Odessa TX 79761

KJ7OT
Ryan M Neary
4775 Oakwood Dr Apt 403
Odessa TX 79761

KE5WQA
Audrey A Davidson
4775 Oakwood Dr Apt 515
Odessa TX 79761

KD5KZR
Jarod K Wilson
2217 Oleander
Odessa TX 79703

KD5RAX

Jarod K Wilson
2217 Oleander
Odessa TX 79703

KE5NPF
Roy J Ward
2107 Pagewood Ave
Odessa TX 79761

KB5MM
Joe D Melton
2114 Pagewood Ave
Odessa TX 79761

KB5RRW
Olen D Baker
2407 Park Blvd
Odessa TX 79763

KD5CWP
Joshua W Jackson
1621 Petroleum
Odessa TX 79762

KF5LRD
Katherine F Malone
17 Pinon
Odessa TX 79765

KF5AEI
Robert A Jones
4000 Pleasant Ave
Odessa TX 79764

N5BNS
Edward L Roskelley
4000 Rasco
Odessa TX 79764

KE5ESO
James Ballin
2906 Redbud
Odessa TX 79762

KC5PAW
John F Mc Ahon
4221 Redbud
Odessa TX 79762

KB5YCB
Christopher K Johnson
4629 Redbud
Odessa TX 79762

KC5GJO
Paul E Zenger
3632 Redbud Ave
Odessa TX 79762

KF5LUV
Ronald L Woodard
3901 Richardson Dr
Odessa TX 79762

KJ5OV
Joe W Meek
3908 Richmond
Odessa TX 79762

WB5MFX
Jimmy D Golden
6217 Riders Rd
Odessa TX 79762

KJ5LV
Edward J Conrad III
2201 Rocky Ln Rd Apt 807
Odessa TX 79762

KC0JTC
Stephen G Snyder
3500 Rocky Ln Rd C
Odessa TX 79762

KD5VFW
William M Smith
1411 Rosewood
Odessa TX 79761

KA3IDN
James F Mellon
1407 Rosewood Ave
Odessa TX 797612908

KC5ETW
Thomas E Mc Cain
2206 Salinas
Odessa TX 79763

N5UNJ
Reagan D Roper
1401 San Andres Dr No 26
Odessa TX 79763

KC5LRJ
John W Spencer
2612 San Fernando
Odessa TX 79763

KF5AEN
Susan E Rodgers
25 San Marcos
Odessa TX 79765

KB5PUT
John R Watson
2628 Santa Monica
Odessa TX 79763

N5QXJ
Kenneth P Theda
2628 Santa Monica
Odessa TX 79763

K5SJY
Bernard C Butts
3747 Scarlet
Odessa TX 79762

KE5MKE
Celestino R Garcia
1521 South Anderson
Odessa TX 79761

KE5HGJ
Juan E Davila Jr
9564 South Carpenter Ave
Odessa TX 79766

KE5RKF
Michael J Titus
9007 South Hwy 385
Odessa TX 79766

N5OMV
Marcus J Pacheco
1310 South Sam Houston St
Odessa TX 79760

N5JZM
Irene E Le Marr
5221 South Southfork Ave
Odessa TX 79766

KF5GGS
Linda S Wilson
150 South Tripp Ave
Odessa TX 79763

KE5TJW
Dana G Wilson
150 South Tripp Ave

Odessa TX 79763

W5NBC
Jimmy D Le Marr
5221 Southfork Ave
Odessa TX 79766

KD5ONK
Richard L Raymond Jr
4000 Springbrook
Odessa TX 79762

WB5UKA
Michael W Jennings
4118 Springbrook Dr
Odessa TX 797628028

KD5WPC
Michael D Tacker
1428 Spur
Odessa TX 79761

KI5AL
John P Hadley
4022 Stillwood Ln
Odessa TX 79762

KD5HAD
James A Martin
7046 Tobosa Ave
Odessa TX 79765

KD5IGV
Sarah M Martin
7046 Tobosa Ave
Odessa TX 79765

KE5ZIX
Rodney J Garrison
835 Tower Dr 14
Odessa TX 79761

KC5NXJ
Donald L Clark
1420 Tulip Ln
Odessa TX 797612913

KC5SDU
Connie E Clark
1420 Tulip Ln
Odessa TX 797612913

KD5JWG
David L Blalock

5404 Veranda Ct
Odessa TX 79762

N5KOA
Leslie C Blalock
5404 Veranda Ct
Odessa TX 79762

KD4LXC
William C Taylor Sr
1435 Verde Ave
Odessa TX 79761

KB5MWW
Samuel W Howell II
7 Versailles Cir
Odessa TX 79760

KC5MDL
Samuel W Howell III
7 Versailles Cir
Odessa TX 79762

N5HBT
Darlene J Covington
4409 Village Way
Odessa TX 79762

N5MW
Michael W Covington
4409 Village Way
Odessa TX 79762

WA5PWF
Marjorie M Lutz
130 Vista Plaza
Odessa TX 79762

KD5SP
Thomas D Shapiro
2111 Wedgewood
Odessa TX 79761

WB5MFV
Gene C Thurber
3601 West 15th
Odessa TX 79763

N3FOX
Roger B Fox
8120 West 18th St
Odessa TX 79763

KC5NDP

Wesley J Stephens
1212 West 20th
Odessa TX 79763

W5SHL
John H Biggs
710 West 21 St
Odessa TX 79763

KD5NFB
Matt S Muehlbrad
604 West 22nd
Odessa TX 79761

KD5IRC
David J Johnson
410 West 22nd St
Odessa TX 79761

W5NQH
David J Johnson
410 West 22nd St
Odessa TX 79761

NI5U
Leon Elms
1608 West 24th
Odessa TX 79763

KD5ADK
Scott A Walker
1807 West 24th St
Odessa TX 797632104

N5OBY
Dennis R Wilson
10670 West 25th
Odessa TX 79763

KA5TXR
James P Banks
9473 West 25th St
Odessa TX 79763

KM5YG
James P Banks
9473 West 25th St
Odessa TX 79763

W5GUD
Norval J Norman
614 West 31st St
Odessa TX 79762

KI5AM
Horace C Freeman
908 West 38th St
Odessa TX 79764

W5GBS
Laney E Huggins
311 West 4th
Odessa TX 79761

K5KDI
Kenneth T Harris Mr
11206 West 63rd
Odessa TX 79764

N5XXN
James R Gideon
11208 West 63rd
Odessa TX 79764

KB5RTT
Kenneth T Harris
11206 West 64th
Odessa TX 79764

KE5DYX
Andrew R Kennedy
9608 West 65th St
Odessa TX 79764

KD5BHP
Kenneth H Hedger
2623 West 81 St
Odessa TX 797641701

KD5QCL
Jerry G Parsons
715 West 81st St
Odessa TX 79764

N5FOI
Thomas J Cronick Sr
2010 West 8th St
Odessa TX 79763

KA5ZGI
Richard L Raymond
4570 West Avocado St
Odessa TX 79766

WB5ZQM
Harry L Raymond
4580 West Avocado St
Odessa TX 79763

N5ETI
John H Davis
311 West Clements
Odessa TX 79761

N5PSP
Alton L Teague
13801 West Co Rd 178
Odessa TX 79766

KD5QEG
Tim J Hackley
13801 West CR 178
Odessa TX 79766

N5SBC
Alicia P Teague
13801 West CR 178
Odessa TX 79766

W5HMR
Tim J Hackley
13801 West CR 178
Odessa TX 79766

KE5F
Alicia P Fuller
13801 West CR 178
Odessa TX 797668710

KD5QIK
John M Patterson
5534 West Cross St
Odessa TX 79763

NG5W
Donald L Potter
12061 West Hoffman
Odessa TX 79764

KD5NMH
Vitale A Justice
11072 West Kassnar Dr
Odessa TX 79764

KD5OKX
Pamela J Justice
11072 West Kassnar Dr
Odessa TX 79764

KC5QIV
Daniel A Toothman
900 West Yukon 66

Odessa TX 79764

KE5OCL
Lawrence C Phillips
2620-B West Yukon Rd
Odessa TX 79764

WB5KWX
Richard V Triplett
1349 Westbrook
Odessa TX 79761

KB5ZND
Rick J Brigman
2201 Westwood Rd 20
Odessa TX 79763

KB5RRV
Kyle D Watts
3009 Windsor
Odessa TX 79762

KD5UEV
Kyle D Watts
3009 Windsor
Odessa TX 79762

K5WJI
Kerry M Ponder
Odessa TX 79768

KD5VFV
Joaquin C Iniguez
Odessa TX 79768

KE5KWP
Joseph L Edwards
Odessa TX 79768

KE5MKD
Jonathan L Edwards
Odessa TX 79768

KE5WJI
Kerry M Ponder
Odessa TX 79768

KD5FL
Sim D Riley
Odessa TX 79769

WD5EJY
Jerry L Gresham
Odessa TX 79764

WB8KVL
Stephen M Nichols
Odessa TX 79768

WB5ZOU
Jamie A Imel
Odessa TX 797682446

FCC Amateur Radio Licenses
in Pecos

N5UEP
Joe W Garrison
1901 Jefferson
Pecos TX 79772

WA5ZBX
Grady T Smith
1413 Johnson St
Pecos TX 79772

WB5HWJ
Charles E Allison Jr
514 Palm Box 255
Pecos TX 79772

K5FLD
Kenneth L Neal
1803 South Alamo St
Pecos TX 79772

KF5DOV
Martin G Villanueva
1118 South Cypress
Pecos TX 79772

KB5IIR
Robert L Spivey
2409 South Eddy
Pecos TX 79772

KE5PPN
Mamie M Clary
1315 West 7th St
Pecos TX 79772

N5RDM
Tommy W Hooker
1402 West 8th
Pecos TX 79772

KE5PPM
Kathleen P Hurley

Pecos TX 79772

KF5IXU
Joe N Villalobos
Pecos TX 79772

FCC Amateur Radio Licenses
in Rankin

W5VEL
Robert W Bradley
1001 Severn St
Rankin TX 79778

FCC Amateur Radio Licenses
in Salt Flat

KD5YIF
Charles A Heil III
HC 60 Box 315
Salt Flat TX 79847

KV4FM
Dennis L Kirk
87620 US Hwy 62 180
Salt Flat TX 79847

N5FMC
George H Temple
Salt Flat TX 79847

FCC Amateur Radio Licenses
in San Elizario

KB5DKS
Enrique I Maese
12878 Socorro Rd
San Elizario TX 79849

KB5HIC
Gerardo R Dena
San Elizario TX 79849

KB5HID
Alma I Pena
San Elizario TX 79849

KB5RMC
Hector Vargas
San Elizario TX 79849

FCC Amateur Radio Licenses
in Sanderson

KE5QEP
Amelia R Lomas
410 Mansfield Box 856
Sanderson TX 79848

AD5BY
John L Sanders
PO Box 114
Sanderson TX 79848

KC5FKA
Martha C Johnson
Sanderson TX 79848

KD5HYB
Amy J Carman
Sanderson TX 79848

KE5QEQ
James T Poe
Sanderson TX 79848

FCC Amateur Radio Licenses
in Sheffield

KB5AKT
Joshua L Klassen
772 New Mexico Ave
Sheffield TX 79781

KD5QCM
Ralph D Houck
Sheffield TX 797810231

FCC Amateur Radio Licenses
in Sherwood

KE5OYC
Joseph M Zeiler
300 Indianhead Cv -28
Sherwood TX 77120

FCC Amateur Radio Licenses
in Sierra Blanca

KB5KWX
Lonny L Hillin
101 Argim
Sierra Blanca TX 79851

KC5DSH
George A Stith
Sierra Blanca TX 79851

KD7BNC
Randy L Coffman
Sierra Blanca TX 79851

FCC Amateur Radio Licenses
in Socorro

KC8HZN
Kenneth R D Norris
725 Delhi Dr
Socorro TX 79927

FCC Amateur Radio Licenses
in Sterling City

KC5DIP
Joshua Z Sides
Box 1026 13Th
Sterling City TX 76951

WI5N
Ralph M Sides
Sterling City TX 76951

AA5SN
Ralph M Sides
Sterling City TX 76951

N5FTL
Royal D Ferguson
Sterling City TX 76951

FCC Amateur Radio Licenses
in Terlingua

KD5LTV
Glenn Rothelle Jr
HC 70
Terlingua TX 79852

KB5ROB
Richard L Keeffe
Terlingua TX 79852

KB5SJU
Steven M Brennecke
Terlingua TX 79852

KC2ARK
Joanne B Arbogast
Terlingua TX 79852

KD5BXC

Karen R Reimers
Terlingua TX 79852

KG6EHE
Patricia E Pollard
Terlingua TX 79852

KG6EHF
Robert V Pollard
Terlingua TX 79852

N1VZL
Willard M Burt
Terlingua TX 79852

WD9CQE
Richard Brotherhood
Terlingua TX 79852

K5VA
Jon S Blackmon
HC70 Hwy 70
Terlinqua TX 79852

**FCC Amateur Radio Licenses
in Toyah**

KB5NMM
Charles D SwiFort Jr
101 South Dubois
Toyah TX 79785

**FCC Amateur Radio Licenses
in Valentine**

KB5YVI
Sergio Moya
Valentine TX 79854

**FCC Amateur Radio Licenses
in Van Horn**

WB5KDQ
Henry I Schaffer
100 10th St
Van Horn TX 79855

KF5GHS
Brandon S Brewster
Van Horn TX 79855

WD5COG
Glenn A Humphries
Van Horn TX 79855

**FCC Amateur Radio Licenses
in Water Valley**

WA0NTX
Eric G Wilkinson
Water Valley TX 76958

KE6ZCB
Terrence R Kummet
Water Valley TX 769580008

**FCC Amateur Radio Licenses
in Wickett**

KA5GIO
Cecil L Dain
Wickett TX 79788

**FCC Amateur Radio Licenses
in Wink**

KE5ZLH
Cendy S Brister Antley
Wink TX 79789